Happiness and External Goods in *Nicomachean Ethics*

Happiness and External Goods in *Nicomachean Ethics*

Sorin Sabou

☙PICKWICK *Publications* · Eugene, Oregon

HAPPINESS AND EXTERNAL GOODS IN *NICOMACHEAN ETHICS*

Copyright © 2019 Sorin Sabou. All rights reserved. Except for brief quotations in critical publications or reviews, no part of this book may be reproduced in any manner without prior written permission from the publisher. Write: Permissions, Wipf and Stock Publishers, 199 W. 8th Ave., Suite 3, Eugene, OR 97401.

Pickwick Publications
An Imprint of Wipf and Stock Publishers
199 W. 8th Ave., Suite 3
Eugene, OR 97401

www.wipfandstock.com

PAPERBACK ISBN: 978-1-5326-9362-5
HARDCOVER ISBN: 978-1-5326-9363-2
EBOOK ISBN: 978-1-5326-9364-9

Cataloguing-in-Publication data:

Names: Sabou, Sorin.

Title: Happiness and external goods in Nicomachean ethics / Sorin Sabou.

Description: Eugene, OR: Pickwick Publications, 2019 | Includes bibliographical references.

Identifiers: ISBN 978-1-5326-9362-5 (paperback) | ISBN 978-1-5326-9363-2 (hardcover) | ISBN 978-1-5326-9364-9 (ebook)

Subjects: LCSH: Aristotle—Nicomachean ethics | Aristotle—Contribution to the concept of happiness | Ethics, Ancient | Happiness—History

Classification: B430.A5 S23 2019 (paperback) | B430.A5 (ebook)

Manufactured in the U.S.A.   09/05/19

for Simona, Andra, and Dora

CONTENTS

CHAPTER 1
INTRODUCTION | 1

CHAPTER 2
HAPPINESS AND EXTERNAL GOODS—AN INTRICATE RELATIONSHIP | 5

CHAPTER 3
SCHOLARLY SOLUTIONS | 20

CHAPTER 4
THE POLITICAL SELF-SUFFICIENCY OF HAPPINESS | 45

CHAPTER 5
AN ENHANCING INSTRUMENTAL DEPENDENCY | 60

CHAPTER 6
A CONSTITUTIVE DEPENDENCY | 72

CHAPTER 7
PRIAM'S LOSSES AND HAPPINESS | 103

CHAPTER 8
AN ANTHROPOLOGICAL DEPENDENCY | 113

CHAPTER 9
CONCLUSION | 129

Bibliography | 135

CHAPTER 1

INTRODUCTION

THIS PROJECT EXPLORES THE topic of dependency of happiness on external goods in *Nicomachean Ethics* (from now on, *EN*). Happiness, as understood by Aristotle in *EN*, is a complex and debated topic, being developed across several books. Happiness is defined by Aristotle as the ultimate good of man, as the self-sufficient good of the ruling science of Politics, as the activity of the soul according to virtue (*EN* I.7). And this ultimate political good is in need of external goods, such as friends, wealth, political power, etc. This dependency of happiness upon goods external to the soul is the topic of this project.

1.1 THESIS

In this project, my thesis to defend is this: the dependency of happiness on external goods, in *EN*, is interpreted in the light of the political self-sufficiency of happiness. The political self-sufficiency of happiness means that, the ultimate good of man, the good of the ruling science of Politics, is self-sufficient based on the self-sufficiency of the city. According to Aristotle, every human being, by nature, is political. The nature of every human being is fundamentally relational. We are what we are, among and with others in the city/πόλις. This constitutive political human nature functions best only in the city. Based on this political anthropology I interpret the dependency of the human political good on external goods in *EN*.

This dependency, I argue, is mainly of three types: (1) enhancing-instrumental, (2) constitutive, and (3) subsistent.

(1) The political good, happiness, depends on external goods of friends, wealth, and political power, both for performing virtuous activities and for self-enhancing. With the help of these political and material goods, happiness performs various virtuous activities in the city and self-enhances its character. These external goods are political external goods needed for promoting the well-being of the city and at the same time for enhancing the virtuous character of the virtuous happy man.

(2) The political good, happiness, depends on external goods of good birth, good children, and beauty because these external goods are constitutive of the political human nature. The political nature of every human being is constituted by our relationships with our prestigious honorable lineage, by our relationships with our good children, and by our enduring beauty at every stage of life. Only when such constitutive elements of our good political nature are absent, our blessedness is ruined. Our blessedness is marred because our political humanity is lacking fundamental relational constituents. The chances for the political good to be possible in human life diminish considerably when someone is utterly ugly, of low-birth, childless, and alone in the world, or even less so when he has bad children or friends, or his children and friends were good, but have died. When these political external goods are absent or lost, the political good, happiness, is not possible. This is so, mainly because our political humanity is dismantled; we have lost constitutive fundamental items of what we are.

(3) The political good, happiness of the intellect, which is separate from the body, still depends on the external goods of a healthy body and food, because our human nature, which is political and composite (body and soul), is not self-sufficient. We are, at the same time, human beings able to contemplate, and in need of a healthy body, food, and other services, to stay alive.

1.2 ROAD MAP

This thesis is defended by following the road map of a detailed argument. So, in chapter 2, I present the three main sets of texts which constitute the textual data for my study. These texts offer the elements of the inquiry, the tensions between various elements within it, and how I am going to analyze them. This textual data needs to be interpreted against the overall picture

INTRODUCTION

of the two main topics: happiness and external goods. That is why, I present an overall understanding of how Aristotle explains and refines his interpretation of happiness, the political good, in *EN*, and then, how he explains the external goods as mainly goods external to the soul. I close chapter 2 by discussing important questions that needs to be addressed in order to understand how happiness depends on external goods in *EN*.

In chapter 3, I present various solutions proposed by the main experts in the field. I organize their interpretations in two main groups where their understanding of what kind of ultimate good happiness is, is decisive for how they interpret the role of the external goods. The scholars who interpret happiness as a monistic good come first and their work is presented in historical order, and then I offer a synthesis of this "monistic interpretation." Then, I present, in historical order, the second group of scholars who interpret happiness as an inclusive good, and how they interpret the role of the external goods. I offer then, a synthesis of this "inclusivist interpretation." I close chapter 3 by presenting the thesis of my project in the light of the present state of representative research.

In chapter 4, I present my interpretation of the meaning of self-sufficiency of happiness. I argue for a political understanding of the self-sufficiency of happiness. This means that the self-sufficiency of happiness is based on the self-sufficiency of the city. This political interpretation of the self-sufficiency of happiness has at its core a political anthropology. According to Aristotle, by nature every human being is a political being. When it comes to self-sufficiency, Aristotle argues that a family, a group, or a city are more self-sufficient than a single individual. The best place for a human being to thrive is the city. This political self-sufficiency of happiness is fundamental for the way in which I interpret the meaning of its dependency on external goods.

In chapter 5, I present my interpretation of the instrumental dependency of happiness on external goods. Friends, wealth, and the political power are mainly political goods. They are the necessary equipment or conditions for practicing political virtues or performing fine acts for the well-being of the city. At the same time, this performing of the noble actions enhances the character of the happy person who does them. For example, the performance of just actions will enhance the virtue of justice in the character of the person who does them.

In chapter 6, I present my interpretation of the constitutive dependency of happiness on external goods. The external goods of good birth/

low birth, good children/bad children, beauty/utterly ugly, good friends/ bad friends are ultimately constitutive goods of the political nature of humanity. When these constitutive goods are absent or lost, our political humanity is dismantled and our blessedness is marred, and our happiness is hardly possible, if not impossible.

In chapter 7, I test this interpretation of understanding the external goods as constitutive of our political nature by studying what happened to Priam, the last king of Troy. This person loses his family, his friends, his wealth, and his city. His political humanity is dismantled, that is why his happiness hardly possible, if not lost. He is still virtuous, as his actions show, but for his happiness to be rebuild a long time would have been needed. He did not have it, as he was killed by Achilles's son.

In chapter 8, I present my interpretation of the subsistent dependency of happiness on external goods. In *EN* X.6–8, Aristotle returns to the main theme of happiness and explains how his inquiry reaches its completion. The complete happiness, contemplation is the happiness of the intellect. This is separate from the body. Even in this case of separatedness from the body, happiness still needs external goods, because on the whole our political human nature is not self-sufficient, it needs a healthy body, food and other services for staying alive. Someone needs to be alive to be able to contemplate; for an embodied soul as we are, we need at least a healthy body and some food to be able to do it.

Chapter 9 is the conclusion of the project. In it, I gather all insights made along the way of this road map and present my interpretation of the dependency of happiness on external goods in *EN*. As I have already said, this dependency needs to be explained starting with a political understanding of the self-sufficiency of happiness and of our human nature. In *EN*, this dependency is mainly enhancing-instrumental and constitutive, but also subsistent.

Now that the main road map is known to the reader, let us start walking and study it in detail and dialogue with others.

CHAPTER 2

HAPPINESS AND EXTERNAL GOODS—AN INTRICATE RELATIONSHIP

2.1 TEXTUAL DATA

THIS STUDY IS ABOUT happiness and the external goods in *EN*. Happiness and external goods in *EN* are a complex topic because these two elements of happiness and external goods are conceived in ways that are not easy to interpret. This is so, because there are several main tensions in what Aristotle says about them in *EN*. I quote below the main textual witness to these tensions. Texts (A) say this:

> If [15] this is the case, human good turns out to be activity of soul in conformity with excellence, and if there are more than one excellence, in conformity with the best and most complete. But we must add "in a complete life." For one swallow does not make a summer, nor does one day; and so too one day, or a short time, does not make a man blessed and happy. Let this serve as an outline of the good; for we must presumably first sketch it [20] roughly, and then later fill in the details. (*EN* I.7, 1098a15–20, Ross and Urmson)

> Now goods have been divided into three classes, and some are described as external, others as relating to soul or to body; and we

call those that relate to soul most properly and truly goods. But we are [15] positing actions and activities relating to soul. Therefore, our account must be sound, at least according to this view, which is an old one and agreed on by philosophers. It is correct also in that we identify the end with certain actions and activities; for thus it falls among goods of the soul and not among external goods. (*EN* I.8, 1098b13–18, Ross and Urmson)

Texts (B) say this:

Yet evidently, as we said, it needs the external goods as well; for it is impossible, or not easy, to do noble acts without the proper equipment. In many actions we use friends and riches and political power as instruments; and there are [1099b1] some things the lack of which takes the lustre from blessedness, as good birth, satisfactory children, beauty; for the man who is very ugly in appearance or ill-born or solitary and childless is hardly happy, and perhaps a man would be still less so if he had thoroughly bad children or friends or had lost good children or friends by [5] death. As we said, then, happiness seems to need this sort of prosperity in addition; for which reason some identify happiness with good fortune, though others identify it with excellence. (*EN* I.8, 1099a30–1099b8, Ross and Urmson)

[25] The answer to the question we are asking is plain also from the definition; for it has been said to be a certain kind of activity of soul. Of the remaining goods, some are necessary, and others are naturally co-operative and useful as instruments. And this will be found to agree with what we said at the outset; for we stated the end of [30] political science to be the best end, and political science spends most of its pains on making the citizens to be of a certain character, viz. good and capable of noble acts. (*EN* I.9, 1099b25–33, Ross and Urmson)

Texts (C) say this:

Being connected with the [20] passions also, the moral excellences must belong to our composite nature; and the excellences of our composite nature are human; so, therefore, are the life and the happiness which correspond to these. The excellence of the intellect is a thing apart; we must be content to say this much about it, for to describe it precisely is a task greater than our purpose requires. It would seem, however, also to need external [25] equipment but little, or less than moral excellence does. (*EN* X.8, 1178a20–25, Ross and Urmson)

> But, being a man, one will also need external prosperity; for our nature is not self-sufficient for the purpose of contemplation, but our body also must be healthy and must have food and other attention. Still, we must not think that the man who is to be happy will need many things or great things, merely because he cannot be [1179a1] blessed without external goods. (*EN* X.8, 1178b33–1179a1, Ross and Urmson)

These texts, (A), (B), and (C), play a decisive role in how the relationship between happiness and the external goods is understood. In texts (A), Aristotle's inquiry about happiness reaches an important signpost at the end of the function argument in *EN* I.7: "human good turns out to be activity of soul in conformity with excellence" (*EN* I.7, 1098a15, Ross and Urmson). Aristotle tells the reader that this definition should "serve as an outline of the good; for we must presumably first sketch it roughly, and the later fill in the details" (*EN* I.7, 1098a19–20, Ross and Urmson). But, when Aristotle inquiries about the goods (which are of three types: of the soul, of the body, and external [*EN* I.8, 1098b13–14]) and how they are relevant for the human good, he says that "we identify the end with certain actions and activities; for thus, it falls among goods of the soul and not among external goods" (*EN* I.8, 1098b19, Ross and Urmson).

These important texts (A) seem to convey the following divergent points about the relationship between happiness and the external goods: on the one hand,

(1) Happiness is just one type of good (activity in accordance with virtue/excellence), and that is why, the external goods are not part of it.

(2) Happiness, as the activity of the soul according to excellence, is only the primary component of happiness that needs to be further explained with details, just as a rough sketch is later on explained more; this seems to be done later in *EN* I.10 where Aristotle says that the happy person is someone "whose activities accord with complete virtue, with an adequate supply of external goods" (*EN* I.10, 1101a16, Irwin).

And, on the other hand:

(3) Happiness is a good of the soul, not an external good, and that is why, the external goods are not included in it.

(4) Happiness, as the ultimate end of man, is primarily a good of the soul, but, according to Aristotle in *EN*, (a) because we are political creatures, our nature is to live with others (*EN* IX.9, 1169b16–20), so, the ultimate good of man is political in nature, and (b) the goods that are relevant

for happiness are mainly the goods that are pursued on their own, in their own right, such as prudence, seeing, pleasure, honor, and the other goods are the goods that are pursued because of these (*EN* IX.9, 1096b16–19).[1]

In texts (B), happiness needs the external goods. There are two reasons for this. (1) There is an instrumental need through which happiness as a virtuous activity can be practiced. To do fine acts, the happy person needs the proper equipment or conditions such as, friends, wealth and political power. (2) There is a non-instrumental need according to which the absence of the external goods has an impact upon blessedness, and the lack of other external goods makes happiness very unlikely; thus, the external goods are necessary for happiness, in such a way that without them, happiness is a distant possibility.

Thus, in texts (B) the dependency of happiness on external goods can be explained mainly in two ways: (1) the dependency of happiness upon external goods is an instrumental dependency to practice virtue, or (2) is a dependency of necessity that makes happiness possible only when some external goods are present. These two main alternatives depend on, the texts (B) say, what the (final) definition of happiness is in *EN* I: (1) if happiness is just one type of good, activity of the soul according to virtue (*EN* I.7), the external goods are not part of it, and happiness is not directly dependent on them, and (2) if the revised definition of happiness includes the external goods as components of happiness, happiness is directly dependent on them.

In texts (C), contemplation as the happiness of the intellect is, on the one hand, a thing apart from the body, and on the other hand, depends on external prosperity such as a healthy body, food, and other services. So, in what way this separatedness of the happiness of the intellect from the body needs to be understood? If the intellect and the body are separable, what are the terms of happiness/contemplation's dependency upon the body? There are two possibilities: (1) the external bodily goods of health and food are needed because they reflect our pleasure for these necessities of life, or (2) they are valuable because human life depends on them.

As I identified the tensions and the things that need to be addressed, now I need to provide an overall understanding of these two things that I study about in *EN*: happiness and external goods. Whatever the path an

---

1. "Honor, pleasure, understanding, and every virtue we certainly choose because of themselves, since we could choose each of them even if it had no further result; but we also choose them for the sake of happiness, supposing that through them we should be happy" (*EN* I.7, 1097b2–4, Ross and Urmson).

interpreter chooses to go, s/he needs to master the whole picture of what Aristotle thinks about these two topics: happiness and external goods. That is why in the next two sections I will provide a bird's eye view upon them, first one about happiness, and then one about external goods.

2.2 ARISTOTLE'S ETHICAL INQUIRY ABOUT HAPPINESS

In this section, I will present the overall line of inquiry about happiness in *EN*.[2] I will highlight the main moves and topics addressed by Aristotle, and how the reader needs to understand them in the *EN*. I will argue that (1) Aristotle begins with an introduction to his subject by presenting it in teleological and political terms. Then, (2) he will inquire about the nature of happiness, and will say that happiness is the ultimate good, the good in itself, the self-sufficient good. Next, (3) Aristotle will search for a more precise explanation of happiness by studying the function of man. To this, (4) he will add an inquiry into the human goodness, and then, (5) he will complete his study of the function of man by inquiring about the highest virtue which is the virtue of the highest part of us, the intellect. This overall structure of Aristotle's entire study in *EN* about happiness is presented in a summary below and will constitute the conceptual background for how happiness is understood in this project.

2.2.1 An Introduction to the Good

The main subject of Aristotle's ethical inquiry in *EN* is happiness, the ultimate end of humans. Right from the start, Aristotle positions his inquiry within a teleological perspective. He observes that whatever a human does, that activity has an end in view (*EN* I.1, 1094a1). He says that, this end or aim is some good. This teleological perspective orders the entire inquiry that follows. The entire search is a search for the ultimate end or the supreme good (*EN* I.2, 1094a20).

This search is a scientific search because the supreme good is the object of every science,[3] especially of the science of Politics, which, according to Aristotle, is the ruling science, the science with most authority (*EN* I.2,

---

2. For the most recent study about the structure of entire *EN*, see Hughes, *Routlege Guidebook*, 8–18.

3. Aristotle understands the term "science" as "the most rigorous sort of discursive knowledge" (Groarke, "Aristotle: Logic").

1094a25). This affirmation makes Aristotle's inquiry a political study. This is so, because the science of Politics is the science that constitutes the apex of all scientific study, and according to Aristotle, the aim of this science is an aim, he claims, that includes the ends of all sciences (*EN* I.2, 1094b5). Aristotle understands the science of Politics in *EN*, as the "most authoritative of the sciences" (*EN* I.2, 1094b28). This means that the science of Politics orders what sciences and what faculties (strategy, economy, oratory, etc.) are needed in the city (*EN* I.2, 1094b1). The aims of all of them are included in the aim of the science of Politics.

This supreme good is ultimately the good of the state. When Aristotle discusses the good of the individual and the good of the state, he says that, the good of the state is greater and more perfect (*EN* I.2, 1094b10). This greatness is due to the fact that is harder to achieve and preserve. When it is achieved, this is seen as a noble and divine achievement. "Divinity" here does not point in the direction of religion, but in the direction of metaphysics. To resemble the gods, for Aristotle, means to get closer to your actuality. Actuality is understood as the fulfillment of human potentiality. Humans in their lives together achieve something of their actuality by securing the good of the state.

But such an ethical inquiry is by no means precise. It is uncertain (*EN* I.3, 1094b20). The object of study makes it to be like that; to study the good, points the enquirer in various directions. Sometimes good things do not lead to good outcomes. There are situations in which a good thing has bad consequences. For example, a rich person can be ruined by his wealth, or someone who is courageous may lose his life when he acts with courage (*EN* I.3, 1094b20). Even when premises are uncertain, and we have to be content with a broad conclusion that depicts the truth (*EN* I.3, 1094b20), the conclusions are right.

When the end of the science of Politics is studied, the person who investigates it must be a well-educated person. Such a person also needs the experience of life. Because of this, a young person is not fit to be a student of Politics. His/her experience of life, according to Aristotle, is incipient and the feelings are in control of his/her life (*EN* I.3, 1095a5). To study Politics is not about acquiring knowledge but understanding the action to be accomplished.

2.2.2 The Finality of Happiness

Aristotle continues his inquiry by discussing about the highest good that can be achieved through action (*EN* I.4, 1095a15). From the way he chooses to speak about the good as the highest good it can be seen that his political teleological ethics is oriented upward, towards the "highest" good. He says that, there is no debate concerning the name of this highest good; everyone speaks about it as happiness [εὐδαιμονία] (*EN* I.4, 1095a20). The disputed thing about the highest good, happiness is "what constitutes it?"

Aristotle's argument in identifying what happiness is, starts with an inquiry about the good. He observes that there are many good things and beyond them there is a good that is "good in itself" and this good is the "cause" of all other things as being good (*EN* I.4, 1095a30). The fact that a thing is good in itself is something proper to it and this feature cannot be taken away easily (*EN* I.5, 1095b29).

This insight is based on a metaphysical principle that says: the "first principle is the fact that a thing is so" (*EN* I.4, 1095b5). This is explained by Aristotle in terms of a student who studies Politics and needs to be very well trained in his habits. Because of this training, a good student of Politics knows already the first principles. This insight brings forward the long discourse about the virtues accomplished by habituation that will follow beginning with the end of Book II in *EN*.

Some good things are called so, by way of proportion (*EN* I.6, 1096b30). For example, a comparison: as sight is good in the human body, so the intelligence is good in the human soul (*EN* I.6, 1096b30). Something is called good because contributes to the good of other things, sight to the body, intelligence to the soul. Aristotle's point is focused on what later, in Book X, will be explained as the "best part" of us and he will study the virtue of this part. He studies the happiness of humans, and this insight about the good, by way of proportion, gives the reader the element which will come under scrutiny at the end of inquiry, the human intellect.

Then, Aristotle continues his teleological practicable inquiry and explains that the good is the aim and reason of all our activities. We do everything for its sake (*EN* I.7, 1097a15), there is nothing beyond it, it is final (*EN* I.7, 1097a30). For example, the acquiring of wealth is not a good in itself, we are doing it because through wealth we can do or have other goods. But the supreme good is a good pursued as an end in itself, it is final, it is never a means towards some other good. Aristotle says that this is what type of good, happiness is. It is a good we always choose for its own sake[4] and never as a means to something else (*EN* I.7, 1097b1).

The same is true in relation to the "self-sufficiency of happiness." Aristotle speaks about "self-sufficiency" as being linked to oneself, and also to others. By nature, every human is a social being (*EN* I.7, 1097b15) who lives with others. But something is self-sufficient when it stands by itself having life desirable and lacking in nothing (*EN* I.7, 1097b15). Because of its finality and self-sufficiency, Aristotle says, happiness is the end towards which all actions aim (*EN* I.7, 1097b20).[5] Thus, the criterion of finality to understand happiness is about being the ultimate end, being the good of the state, an end in itself, not a means towards something else, it is about being self-sufficient.

2.2.3 Function of Man

Aristotle continues his ethical inquiry because he needs a more explicit understanding of what constitute happiness (*EN* I.7, 1097b25). He will be able to be more explicit in explaining happiness by finding out what is man's function (*EN* I.7, 1097b25). The criterion of the "function" builds on the criterion of "finality" by exploring what is peculiar to man. Aristotle gives the reader two reasons why he is going to study the function: (1) everything has a function to perform, and (2) the goodness or the efficiency of everything is found in that function (*EN* I.7, 1097b28). For example, every member of the human body has some function: the ear to hear, the hand to do things, and when this member of the body fulfills its function it is a good member of the body. So, Aristotle has to establish what the function of man is, and then, based on this, he will be able to explain better what the good of man/happiness is.

Aristotle explains the criterion of the function by looking at what is peculiar to humans (*EN* I.7, 1098a1). What is peculiar to every human

---

4. This idea that we do something "for the sake of" happiness is understood by the inclusivist scholars in the following way: "A for the sake of B" means that "A contributes as a constituent to B." The good actions, which are ends in themselves, are constituent to happiness. See Ackrill, "Aristotle on *Eudaimonia*," 72; Irwin, "Permanent Happiness," 10; Annas, "Aristotle on Virtue and Happiness," 36.

5. The inclusivist scholars interpret this architectonic structure of the ultimate political end as the end in which all other ends are included (*EN* I.2, 1094b7; Ackrill, "Aristotle on *Eudaimonia*," 7; Urmson, *Aristotle's Ethics*, 119; Hester, "Aristotle on the Function of Man," 12; Höffe, *Aristotle*, 151).

being is "the practical life of the rational part of man" (*EN* I.7, 1098a3). The ability to exercise one's rational faculty is what Aristotle has in view when talks about rational life. Based on this explanation, the function of man is understood as the activity of the soul in conformity with rational principle (*EN* I.7, 1098a20).[6] When this activity is performed well and rightly, the good man is fulfilling his function. When the faculties of the soul are active in accordance with the rational principle, the human being fulfills his/her function, and when these faculties are active in accordance with excellence (*EN* I.7, 1098a20) s/he is fulfilling the function well. This is how the "good of man" is described by Aristotle with the help of the criterion of the function.

When Aristotle is finished with his exposition of the function criterion, he offers the reader a signpost by saying: "let this account serve to describe the Good in outline." What is understood by this is described by the action of "making a rough sketch" (*EN* I.7, 1098a21).

2.2.4 The Human Goodness

Aristotle will continue to explore the meaning of happiness by examining the "nature of goodness." He has to do this because he defines happiness as the "activity of the soul in conformity with perfect goodness" (*EN* I.13, 1102a5). For Aristotle, the goodness of humans is an "excellence of soul" (*EN* I.13, 1102a25). This is the reason for which everyone who studies politics has to study the soul and its nature (*EN* I.13, 1102a25).

Aristotle presents his understanding of the soul as having two parts ("irrational" and "capable of reason," *EN* I.13, 1102a30), and of virtue as depending on this understanding of the soul: moral and intellectual (*EN* I.13, 1103a5). These two kinds of virtue, moral and intellectual, are studied further and Aristotle says that we, as humans, have the natural ability to develop them, and by habit we develop this ability to maturity (*EN* II.1, 1103a25). This capacity "given by nature" is understood by Aristotle in metaphysical terms. We have these capacities "in a potential form" and we are able to exercise them (*EN* II.1, 1103a30). This is how, in the area of

---

6. The monistic scholars interpret Aristotle's definition of happiness based on the function argument as speaking about one activity of the soul in accordance with virtue, not about an aggregate composed of several actions, virtue and people (Kraut, *Aristotle on the Human Good*, 79, 81; Hardie, "Final Good," 283; Richardson Lear, "Happiness," 397; Kenny, "Happiness," 100; Bush, "Divine and Human Happiness," 50).

virtue, a human can move from potentiality to actuality; this is the basic framework of change in Aristotelian philosophy. When we exercise them, we become more virtuous: "we become just by doing just acts" (*EN* II.1, 1103b30). In other words, certain activities form certain moral dispositions (*EN* II.1, 1103b15).

This relationship between activities and moral dispositions makes Aristotle to inquire into the area of conduct (*EN* II.2, 1103b30). His analysis is detailed (see *EN* II.2, 1103b30–1104b1) and reaches the following conclusion: when we observe the mean [relative to us] we have a stable disposition of our mind and this is a virtue (*EN* II.6, 1107a1). We will position ourselves between all kind of excesses. In Book II of *EN* Aristotle shows the relevancy of "virtue" to his study of happiness. He will expand his inquiry of virtues extensively for several other books, but in Book X he returns to his inquiry of happiness. This is what I will explain in the next subsection.

2.2.5 Contemplation

Aristotle's exposition in Book X.6–9 is the completion of his "function" argument. The completion of the "function" argument is accomplished in the following way: "if happiness consists in activity in accordance with virtue, it is reasonable that it should be activity in accordance with the highest virtue; and this will be the virtue of the best part of us" (*EN* X.7, 1177a15, Rackham). The highest virtue, as the virtue of the best part of us, is the ultimate point in his inquiry into the function of man; it is the best of the best part of us.

Analyzing the activity of the best part of us helps Aristotle to complete his inquiry on happiness.[7] Aristotle identifies the best part of us as being the part that rules, leads, and gives us knowledge of what is noble and divine (*EN* X.7, 1177a15). That part is our intellect. The reference to those

---

7. This point is greatly debated by Aristotelian scholars: is Aristotle speaking about the same thing or about something else, as he used to speak about "happiness" (Books I and II), but now he speaks about "perfect happiness" (Book X). There are scholars who say that Aristotle is consistent and offers a single account of happiness throughout his entire inquiry in *EN* (Cooper, *Reason and Emotion*, 235; Kraut, *Aristotle on the Human Good*, 314; "Aristotle on the Human Good," 90; Van Cleemput, "Aristotle on Happiness," 95; Baracchi, *Aristotle's Ethics*, 96; Richardson Lear, "Happiness," 401), and there are scholars who say that Aristotle works with two accounts of happiness in his inquiry (Curzer, "Criteria for Happiness," 422; *Aristotle & Virtues*, 392, 424; Nagel, "Aristotle on *Eudaimonia*," 252; Bush, "Divine and Human Happiness," 51; Shields, *Aristotle*, 341, 343).

elements (rule, lead, knowledge of noble and divine) can be understood to help Aristotle to reach the ultimate goal of his inquiry. Every human needs the right rule of reason, the practice of what is noble, and to reach the highest possible stage of his/her actuality.

This best part of us, the intellect, has its own proper activity, and when this is done in accordance with its proper virtue or excellence, this activity is the activity of contemplation (*EN* X.7, 1177a20). This reference to "contemplation" is not new because Aristotle already mentioned it (*EN* I.10, 1100b20; IV.2, 1122b17; VII.3, 1146b14).

The fact that, in Book X, Aristotle identifies happiness with contemplation is not a different approach, to that of Books I and II on this subject, but one that is in agreement with the results already accomplished. Also, Aristotle says, it is in agreement with the truth (*EN* X.7, 1177a20). The intellect being the highest thing in us, its activity, contemplation, is the highest activity. Aristotle understands contemplation as being continuous, pleasant, self-sufficient, and loved for its own sake; that is why, it constitutes "complete human happiness" (*EN* X.7, 1177b25).

Contemplation is a life at a higher level because it is the activity of the intellect, which, according to Aristotle, is the divine part of us (*EN* X.7, 1177b30). This affirmation about the life of contemplation as being "higher than human level" has to be explained carefully. It does not mean that is beyond our reach as humans, but it says that, because of the divine element within us, which is our intellect, we, as humans, are able to live higher than human level, we are able to contemplate. This is a life that is not lived at the level of physical needs, but a life lived at the level of our intellect which is the "highest thing in us." Our "composite nature" (human/divine) leads to this differentiation between the life of the intellect and the life of the human being (*EN* X.7, 1177b30).

In *EN* X.7, 1178a5, there is another strong indication that here, in Book X, Aristotle continues his "function" criterion: "That which is best and most pleasant for each creature is that which is proper to the nature of each." This link between "what is best" and "that which is proper to the nature of each" is explored further by Aristotle. The life of the best part of us which is the life of the intellect is the "best and the pleasant life" for us, humans (*EN* X.7, 1178a5). In comparison with this best and most pleasant life, the virtuous moral life is happy only "in a secondary degree" (*EN* X.8, 1178a10). This affirmation means that any virtue that is not intellectual does not reach the highest point. Aristotle makes this distinction based on the way he explains the nature of the soul. When the intellect does not act in a central way that activity will be a moral activity and it will constitute happiness, but in a secondary degree. It is "secondary" because it does not reach the highest possible point for humans. This highest, ultimate point is reached when the intellect, which is the highest thing in us, is active, when it contemplates.

Thus, this is an overview of Aristotle's inquiry about happiness in *EN*, and I will assume it, and use it as the general background when I analyze its relationship to the external goods. In the next section I will present what Aristotle means by external goods as the necessary clarification before interpreting the relationship they have with happiness.

2.3 EXTERNAL GOODS

As I mentioned earlier in chapter 2.1, Aristotle works with an old and agreed division of the goods in three main classes (*EN* I.8, 1098b13).[8] There are goods related to the soul, goods related to the body, and external goods. Aristotle sees the goods of the soul as referring to the activities of the soul. The point that Aristotle makes is that, the ultimate end of man is found among the goods of the soul, and not among the external goods.

Thus, in relation to happiness, the ultimate end of man, Aristotle sees the goods in two general classes: of the soul, and external to the soul. The old and agreed three-way division of the goods is acknowledged, but now reorganized: the goods of the body are treated together with the external goods in one broad class of external goods, and the other class is the goods of the soul. This treatment together of the goods of the body with external goods in one broad class of external goods is seen later in *EN* I.8, 1099a31–1099b8, where external goods like wealth, political power, friends, children are treated together with goods of the body like beauty or the lack of good looks. These two classes of goods (goods of the body and external goods) treated together as external goods are external to the soul.

Such an observation that, the goods of the body and the external goods have to be interpreted together as one broad group of external goods is in agreement with what other scholars say. For example, Cooper sees

---

8. A similar division is mentioned in Aristotle's *Politics* VII.1: "Certainly no one will dispute the propriety of that partition of goods which separates them into three classes, viz. external goods, goods of the body, and goods of the soul, or deny that the happy man must have all three" (*Pol* VII.1, 1323a24–26, Jowett).

this division in two main classes: "the external goods we are talking about are all the good things a person can acquire or enjoy that lie outside his own mind and character (his soul)"[9]; Cashen explains the division of the goods by Aristotle as (1) goods of the soul (virtues of character and intellect) and (2) goods external to the soul (goods of the body like physical fitness and attractiveness, and external goods like wealth, political influence, friendship)[10]; Roche makes a similar observation when he says that "Aristotle is not particularly interested in the distinction between goods of the body and external goods . . . therefore it seems appropriate to take both goods of the body and Aristotle's narrow class of strictly external goods together as one group of goods distinct from the goods of the soul."[11] So, when Aristotle uses the phrase "external goods" in *EN* he assumes this broad class of goods that are external to the soul.

2.4 QUESTIONS AND TENSIONS

In his long and complex ethical inquiry, Aristotle mentions that happiness needs external goods or external prosperity (*EN* I.8, 1099a27; X.8, 1178b32). These statements are the subject of intense research because of the tensions between Aristotle's criteria of completeness and self-sufficiency of happiness, and its need for external goods. The dependency of happiness upon external goods represents a problem whose solution, or the lack of it, depends on how the main items in it are explained. Thus, based on Aristotle's ethical inquiry, happiness is an internal subjective condition in need of external good conditions.

How are these two explained by Aristotle? Aristotle says that "we cannot do fine actions if we lack the resources" (*EN* I.8, 1099a32). He identifies these resources as friends, wealth, and political power. The external goods are the instruments of virtue because virtuous acts are performed with their help.

---

9. Cooper, "Goods of Fortune," 177.
10. Cashen, "Ugly, the Lonely, and the Lowly," 1–2.
11. Roche, "Happiness and External Goods," 37. A somewhat similar understanding of treating together the goods of the body with external goods has Russell when he says that "the things he identifies as bodily and external goods are those that would seem so to anyone: friends, wealth, influence, being well-born, having good children, being attractive" (Russell, *Happiness for Humans*, 108).

But, is there anything else about the external goods in relation to happiness? Do they have any other value in relation to happiness? Aristotle says that, the deprivation of certain externals "mars our blessedness" (*EN* I.8, 1099b1). These externals are: good birth, good children, and beauty. If the lack of these external goods has the ability to mar happiness, it means that they have a different type of value than an external one. It looks like they have somehow an intrinsic value, because, when they are not present, blessedness is ruined. The difficult aspect of this discussion is that something external, such as the lack of good children, has the impact to mar happiness.

How is this to be reconciled with what Aristotle says about the completeness and self-sufficiency of happiness? Happiness has an intrinsic value because of its completeness and self-sufficiency. But now Aristotle says that happiness is not possible for someone of ill birth, ugly, or childless (*EN* I.8, 1099b4). And if our children or friends are bad or dead, we cannot be happy. It looks like the lack of these externals has an intrinsic impact on happiness. If things are in that way, happiness is not possible. That means that they are part of the happiness.[12] This problem/tension is difficult to explain[13] because it endangers the criteria of completeness and self-sufficiency.

And, the human intellect is separable from the body, and so is the happiness of the intellect (X.8, 1078a22). That being so, according to Aristotle, how is it that it needs bodily goods such as health and food? What kind of dependency contemplation has?

So, is Aristotle's ethical inquiry able to reconcile the following problems? (1) When the external goods are lost, happiness is ruined, (2) a happy person cannot be miserable, (3) when someone experiences what king Priam experienced, that person cannot be happy, and (4) when a fine act is done with the help of some external goods (wealth, friends, political power) is the external part of the process through which someone practices virtue and becomes virtuous, or not? (5) Can a separate thing, our intellect, be supported by our body and its goods?

---

12. Altobello puts it this way: "If X's loss is bad because it mars my happiness, then X has instrumental value, but in order for X's loss to mar my happiness X must have intrinsic value. Thus, X must have intrinsic value, but Aristotle cannot give it any" (Altobello, "Five Ancient Theories of Happiness," 32).

13. See also Annas, who says that "Aristotle needs, but has not thought through, a satisfactory account of just how the external goods do figure in the happy life" (Annas, *Morality of Happiness*, 384).

To answer such difficult questions, I need to explain the relationship between the internal and external conditions of happiness. On the internal side of the inquiry, I need to analyze the meaning of completeness and self-sufficiency of happiness. Because it seems that, based on these two criteria, the happiness does not need anything else beyond itself. That is why, an important question is whether the external goods are part of the happiness or not. If they are, in what way, and what is the meaning of self-sufficiency then? On the external side of the inquiry, there are the difficult questions of the dependency of happiness on external goods. For example, if someone is ugly, s/he cannot be fully happy. How would Aristotle apply this insight to Socrates, who was ugly? Or if someone's child has died, how that tragic event impedes his/her happiness? How is that applied to king Priam, who suffered such loss? At what point is happiness dislodged by disaster?

These are the sides of the problem that need to be analyzed and searched for an answer from Aristotle, if there is one. Is Aristotle's understanding of happiness unstable[14] because of the need of external goods, or not, or is only vulnerable?[15] In other words, what is the meaning of dependency of happiness on the external goods? Various scholars answered these questions in various ways. I will present their representative positions in the next chapter.

---

14. The language of instability is famous because of Annas, who says "[Aristotle at times] stresses the importance of the external goods to an extent incompatible with [virtue] and [this] is ultimately unstable" (Annas, *Morality of Happiness*, 384).

15. The language of vulnerability or fragility of the human good in Aristotle is famous because of Nussbaum. See especially Nussbaum, *Fragility of Goodness*, 318–42.

CHAPTER 3

SCHOLARLY SOLUTIONS

3.1 INTRODUCTION

THE TOPIC OF HAPPINESS and external goods is touched upon in every major study about happiness in *EN*; thus, the amount of literature is vast. From this vast scholarly context, I have selected a number of scholars who are seen as representatives of the main interpretative alternatives when it comes to happiness and external goods. For an easy way to remember these alternatives I label them as (1) n-interpretation (the external goods are *not* part of happiness, and happiness does not depend directly on them), and (2) p-interpretation (the external goods are *part* of happiness and happiness depends directly on them). The following scholars and their interpretations belong to (1) monism: Heinaman, Kraut, Cooper, Brown, Cashen,[1] and (2) inclusivism: Cooper, Irwin, Nussbaum, Russell, Roche.[2] Monistic interpreters assume that happiness is a monistic good and inclusive interpreters assume that happiness is an inclusive good. For making this assumption clear at the beginning of the following main sections 3.2 and 3.3, I will

---

1. See Heinaman, "*Eudaimonia* and Self-Sufficiency"; Kraut, *Aristotle on the Human Good*; Cooper, *Knowledge, Nature, and the Good*; Brown, "Wishing for Fortune"; Cashen, "Ugly, the Lonely, and the Lowly."

2. See Cooper, "Aristotle on the Goods of Fortune"; Irwin, "Permanent Happiness"; Nussbaum, *Fragility of Goodness*; Russell, *Happiness for Humans*; Roche, "Happiness and External Goods."

present a concise description of the arguments for happiness as a monistic good or an inclusive good.

These scholars work with different questions when they study the relationship between happiness and external goods, that is why, (1) I will identify what their question(s) are and how they answer it/them, and then (2) I will present a synthesis of them together as they belong to the two main ways of understanding the relationship between external goods and happiness in *EN*. The synthesis will be of great importance as it will serve as an interpretation to be tested and debated in various ways later on in the project.

3.2 MONISM

In this section I will present the contributions brought by the monistic scholars to the ongoing research about the meaning of relationship between happiness and external goods in *EN*. Their interests are varied, and I will focus mainly on their ways of posing the problem and then specifically on their contribution to the debate. The monistic scholars argue that the external goods are not part of happiness, are presented in historical order. I will start by (1) giving a concise summary of how the n-interpretation understands happiness as a monistic good, and then, (2) I will present the five representative scholars. After this presentation, I will (3) put together a summary of the interpretative monistic strategy, and that will constitute my overall summary of this approach and it will be an interlocutor further on in this project.

3.2.1 Happiness as the Monistic Good

The understanding of happiness as a monistic good (also known as the "dominant" interpretation) is explained as follows. The final hierarchical end, for Aristotle, is not an inclusive aggregate but "one type of good."[3] Aristotle's definition of happiness based on the function argument speaks about one activity of the soul in accordance with virtue, not about an aggregate composed of several actions, virtues and people.[4] These are goods

---

3. See Kraut, "Aristotle on the Human Good," 79; Kenny, "Happiness," 100; Richardson Lear, "Happiness," 397; Hardie, "Final Good in Aristotle's Ethics," 283.

4. Kraut, "Aristotle on the Human Good," 81; Bush, "Divine and Human Happiness," 50.

in themselves but the problem with them is that they are not final enough.[5] Virtuous activity is the good of man, and this is one single item, not a composed variety of goods. By virtuous activity Aristotle means the virtuous activity of the soul, not a vast array of activities in the city, which have their own contribution to a superior end.

Aristotle does not add to this activity anything else; happiness for Aristotle is not a state, but an activity only.[6] Virtuous activity as the good of man is not a good among other goods, but the good for the sake of which everything else is done. This virtuous activity of the soul is sustained by other goods (health, people, etc.) but these goods do not add value to it.[7] The end of Aristotle's inquiry identifies this one good as contemplation, the virtuous activity of the rational soul. This is the highest good because is the activity of the highest part of us, our intellect.[8]

3.2.2 R. Heinaman

Heinaman's paper is an argument against the inclusive interpretation of happiness in *EN*. His main focus is on the criterion of self-sufficiency which is understood by the inclusive interpreters as being decisive for their interpretation.[9] In disagreement with Cooper and Irwin, Heinaman says that happiness denotes a certain type of life and not a certain kind of total life of a person; happiness is an intellectual activity.[10]

Heinaman understands the self-sufficiency of happiness as that criterion on which "on its own" happiness makes life desirable and lacking in nothing. Happiness on its own and not in combination with anything else. Moral action on its own and contemplation on its own are self-sufficient.[11] For Aristotle, Heinaman says, happiness is "nothing but the exercise of our rational faculties. So, anything that is not such an activity cannot constitute *eudaimonia*."[12]

---

5. Richardson Lear, "Happiness," 398.
6. Kraut, "Aristotle on the Human Good," 82.
7. Kraut, "Aristotle on the Human Good," 85; Kenny, *Aristotelian Ethics*, 204.
8. Kraut, "Aristotle on the Human Good," 88; Richardson, "Happy Lives and the Highest Good," 7.
9. Heinaman, "*Eudaimonia* and Self-Sufficiency," 31–32.
10. Heinaman, "*Eudaimonia* and Self-Sufficiency," 33.
11. Heinaman, "*Eudaimonia* and Self-Sufficiency," 47.
12. Heinaman, "*Eudaimonia* and Self-Sufficiency," 48.

Heinaman introduces the topic of external goods at the point where he mentions that different people are happy in various degrees. This point is based, according to Heinaman, on varied ability on the part of varied people to engage in contemplation and moral action. But, according to Heinaman, there are other factors such as extreme ugliness and good birth whose presence or absence affect the degree of happiness or its very existence.[13]

This impact of the presence or absence of external goods upon happiness is explained by Heinaman as referring to external goods as necessary conditions of happiness. The fact that they are conditions for happiness, Heinaman says, does not make them components of happiness. The external goods have to be seen as necessary conditions for happiness because their absence is an impediment for the activities that are happiness.[14]

Also, Heinaman argues that happiness cannot include all intrinsic goods because this will go against the conclusion of the function argument. For example, seeing is an intrinsic good (*EN* I.6, 1096b16–19) and seeing is an intrinsically good activity, but based on the function argument, seeing is not included in happiness because seeing is not an ability and a function distinctive of man (*EN* I.7, 1098a1–3). Thus, happiness is not composed of all intrinsic good activities.[15]

3.2.3 R. Kraut

Kraut's exegesis of *EN* I.8 explains how the lack of goods like good birth, good children and beauty mars blessedness in terms of defects in social standing, family and appearance. When someone does not have those goods, that person is less equipped, and the performance of fine activities is no longer possible. So, Kraut argues that Aristotle refers here to the causal role of goods.[16]

When a person has the goods mentioned by Aristotle, Kraut says, those goods are a part of that person's equipment for virtuous activity. By having the proper equipment that person is in an advantageous position to achieve virtuous acts. For example, a person who is in a political position of power has all the advantages of that position: wealth, power, friends, and most likely comes from a prestigious lineage. Such a person with high

---

13. Heinaman, "*Eudaimonia* and Self-Sufficiency," 34.
14. Heinaman, "*Eudaimonia* and Self-Sufficiency," 49.
15. Heinaman, "*Eudaimonia* and Self-Sufficiency," 49.
16. Kraut, *Aristotle on the Human Good*, 254.

social standing and appreciation benefits of an advantageous setting that enhances his influence. By contrast a person who does not have any of these advantages and is ugly, of low birth, without children and with bad friends will be greatly disadvantaged.

Thus, Kraut explanation is in terms of the impact of social standing and attitudes of someone's high or low stock of external goods: if the stock is high, for that person will be easier to perform virtuous actions, but if the stock of external goods is low, for that person will be harder to perform any virtuous actions.[17]

But, according to Kraut, Aristotle provides an even worst-case scenario. If someone has bad children and bad friends, that person is at a greater disadvantage than being solitary or childless. The reason for this is the way social attitudes affect his opportunities for performing fine acts; such a person faces more opprobrium than one who is solitary and without children. The reason for this opprobrium is the damage and the disgrace brought upon him by his bad children and friends.[18]

The fact of death of children and friends is an impediment for virtuous action because of the pain the parent or friend experiences. In times like this of great loss it is very difficult to perform fine acts. To support this point, Kraut mentions what Aristotle says in *EN* X.5, 1175b22–24, that pain destroys activity. Great disasters are painful and block many activities (*EN* I.10, 1100b29–30). So, such a parent who has lost his good children, or a friend who has lost his good friends have lost (1) their resources for doing virtuous acts, and (2) they are overwhelmed by pain and so are impeded to do fine acts.[19]

Kraut explains the role of fortune (good or bad) by focusing, on one hand, on the fact that happiness as the activity of the rational soul in accordance with perfect virtue is achieved through individual effort and not good fortune, and, on the other hand, for supporting regular virtuous activity for a lifetime, resources are needed, and for this fortune is a factor that can decrease them or increase them. When times are good the resources prosper, but when times are bad, they can be lost. In this way, Kraut preserves the distinction between happiness, the ultimate end, as a monistic good and various goods upon which virtuous activity depends.[20]

17. Kraut, *Aristotle on the Human Good*, 255.
18. Kraut, *Aristotle on the Human Good*, 256.
19. Kraut, *Aristotle on the Human Good*, 256.
20. Kraut, *Aristotle on the Human Good*, 257.

The good fortune leads to a greater prominence, attractiveness, more opportunities to achieve virtuous activities, and bad fortune leads to lesser prominence, attractiveness and less opportunities to achieve virtuous activities. This is how happiness is increased through more virtuous activity or destroyed through pain and lack of virtuous activity. So, according to Kraut, happiness is equated with virtuous activity, and the other goods are not its components but the equipment the moral agent needs to attain it.[21]

3.2.4 J. Cooper

In a book published in 2004, J. Cooper seems to have changed his initial inclusive understanding of external goods published in 1985 (see my summary of it in chapter 3.3.2). Cooper's recent monistic interpretation is important because he presents it in the larger context of the meaning of self-sufficiency of happiness in *EN* as it contrasts with that of its sufficiency presented by Plato/Socrates in *Philebus*.

The need of happiness for external goods is explained by Cooper to mean these goods have to be seen as a supplement to happiness. According to Cooper, the external goods are not an addition to virtuous activity, but a supplement to happiness itself. This is a major distinction that situates Cooper somewhere between the interpretation that sees the external goods as conditions needed by *eudaimonia* to be performed (Heinaman), or external goods needed when happiness is fully engaged (Kraut). What Aristotle says here, Cooper states, is that it is not that someone cannot have happiness without these goods as they were included in it as components, because Aristotle already has enounced his understanding of happiness in *EN* I.7 without mentioning these goods as being included in it.[22]

When someone has happiness, that person will need these external goods too. They are further things that are needed. Cooper explains self-sufficiency of happiness here as not including these external goods, that being the reason for which now he says that they are required; for Cooper, happiness is self-sufficient, not sufficient, which means that sufficiency as applied to happiness refers only to its own self-sufficiency, and not to a sufficient overall condition of someone's life. These external goods are not the goods that make happiness choiceworthy, but they are needed for making the life of happiness more satisfactory. In other words, they are things to be

---

21. Kraut, *Aristotle on the Human Good*, 260.
22. Cooper, *Knowledge, Nature, and the Good*, 286.

wished and hope for. They are not important; they are not make-or-break conditions for a life worth choosing; only happiness is important in that way.[23]

So, when these external goods are absent or lacking their absence is not that important because they are needed just to make life more satisfactory. Their absence does not make a life not worth choosing; they are just goods worth desiring and worth being concerned for.[24]

This understanding of self-sufficiency of happiness as referring strictly to its own sufficiency, and not to the total complete condition of a happy life, allows Cooper to interpret the need for external goods to be added to it in terms of things that will improve life if you have them. This is seen even with contemplation is discussed. The contemplation as perfect happiness needs them too. Contemplation does not need them to make virtuous activity possible, but it needs them for remaining alive and active.[25]

3.2.5 E. Brown

According to Brown, Aristotle's understanding of the role of external goods in relation to happiness is discerned by seeking an answer to the following question: "Does Aristotle really mean that the human good is just virtuous rational activity? Are health and wealth, not to mention friends and lovers, *not* part of the goal for the sake of which one should do everything one does?"[26]

Brown answers these questions with the following answers. The main thesis defended by Brown is focused strictly on *EN* I.8 where, Brown says, Aristotle sticks by his narrow account of happiness from *EN* I.7; this stays the same throughout Book I. This thesis is supported by a thorough exegetical study of *EN* I.8–12 where he argues that the external goods are necessary for virtuous activity because virtuous people have a psychological need for certain external goods. Brown says that Aristotle wants that his readers to choose virtuous activity while wishing for good fortune and the external goods brought by it.

This tandem between choosing and wishing is at the core of Brown's interpretation of why the external goods are necessary for virtuous activity.

---

23. Cooper, *Knowledge, Nature, and the Good*, 287.
24. Cooper, *Knowledge, Nature, and the Good*, 288.
25. Cooper, *Knowledge, Nature, and the Good*, 297.
26. Brown, "Wishing for Fortune," 57.

In other words, a virtuous person chooses to practice virtue because s/he wishes for external goods brought by good fortune. These external goods cannot be chosen, only wished for. Brown says that this is so because (1) virtue is constituted by the correct appreciation of value, and (2) our capacity to choose virtuously is diminished when we do not get what we wish for.[27]

Brown clarifies more his interpretation by saying that a virtuous person needs to have certain attitudes in order to have the psychological makeup required for virtue. A virtuous person appreciates correctly what are the things of value and wishes for them. A virtuous person, according to Brown, acts solely for the sake of virtuous activity but she needs to wish for the things s/he values in order to be psychologically capable of virtuous activity. What we have here, Brown says, is an agent who wishes for all sorts of goods for their own sake, but this agent always chooses activity.[28]

2.3.6 M. Cashen

In studying the relationship between virtuous activity of the soul (happiness) and external goods in *EN*, according to Cashen, the interpretative question is this: "Why should any goods external to the soul impact happiness when these have so little to do with character, choice, and action?"[29] Cashen presents and analyses the two interpretative strategies, monism and inclusivism, and he situates in the middle of the debate about them, defending the monist interpretation with new insights.

According to Cashen, the monist interpretation allows Aristotle to do two things: (1) to maintain his identification of happiness with virtue, and (2) to put forward a plausible story of how the deprivation of external goods impacts happiness. Cashen interprets the deprivation of external goods as (1) preventing us from accomplishing what we have set out to do, and (2) as spoiling happiness in virtue of suffering and disappointment it inflicts and their effect upon our character.[30]

---

27. Brown, "Wishing for Fortune," 58.
28. Brown, "Wishing for Fortune," 79–80.
29. Cashen, "Ugly, the Lonely, and the Lowly," 2.
30. Cashen, "Ugly, the Lonely, and the Lowly," 17.

2.3.7 The Monistic Good and the External Goods

These five representatives of the monistic interpretation explored the dependency of happiness upon the external goods in various ways. The two main complex questions are these:

(1) If happiness is just one complete self-sufficient good, and nothing can be added to it to make it greater or better, in what way the external goods need to be added to it?

(2) If happiness is a good of the soul, and not a good of the body or an external good, how is it that the loss of the external goods has an impact upon it, and what the nature of this impact is?

The monistic interpretation answers these difficult questions in the following way.[31] The summary answer to question 1. The self-sufficiency of happiness needs to be understood as referring to the fact that happiness is sufficient on its own, it does not depend on anything else. Happiness as virtuous activity of the rational soul is, on its own, sufficient as being the ultimate end for the sake of which we choose everything else. Happiness on its own, not in combination with anything else, makes life desirable and lacking in nothing. The external goods are added as a supplement to happiness to make life more satisfactory. They are not decisive factors as happiness is to make life choiceworthy.

The external goods are conditions/resources of the self-sufficient good. Happiness is the complete good which means that nothing can be added to it to make it greater or better. The addition of the external goods is not for completing happiness but for practicing virtue. The external goods are only equipment or tools, not parts that are added to make happiness more complete. Thus, when someone chooses to practice virtues, that person appreciates what is of value, and hopes for good fortune and its external goods. The external goods are needed to be added to happiness because when we choose the virtuous activity of the rational soul we hope for better times and its goods.

To be in an advantageous position is the main thing that explains the need for the external goods. Such a person has the necessary equipment. His/her friends, wealth, power, beauty will help to perform noble activities.

---

31. A summary of the monistic interpretation is also provided by Roche who says that "the external goods provide *either* (i) instrumental means (or objects) for the performance of virtuous acts *or* (ii) advantageous conditions for the performance of such acts *or* (iii) freedom from the psychological pain that might interfere with our ability to engage in such acts" (Roche, "Happiness and External Goods," 49).

Being wealthy, powerful, beautiful and having good children are great advantages. Such a person is noticed by others because of these advantages. When someone is of low standing, poor, and ugly does not have prominence among people, and will not have opportunities to do noble acts.

For Aristotle, in *EN*, the main controlling factor in happiness is virtue. And because the practice of virtue needs external goods, happiness needs external goods to be added to it. Virtuous activity controls happiness. Thus, the need for external goods to be added to happiness is explained in terms of resources or conditions for it. The dominance of virtue asks for external goods as tools.

The language of "control" or "dominance" suggests that Aristotle works with a hierarchy of the goods: some are subordinate, and one is the ultimate good. For Aristotle, virtuous activity is the ultimate good which rules the other goods that are subordinate. And, the ultimate end, the virtuous activity of the soul, happiness, is the controlling good. The virtuous activity is the controlling good of the political life, and the contemplation is the controlling good of the perfect happy life. This dominance of virtue is a reason for the need for external goods both in the political life and in perfect happy life.

Thus, in *EN*, external goods are needed as resources for virtuous activity. But in what amount? Aristotle answers that a person needs to be sufficiently equipped with external goods (*EN* I.10, 1101a14–16). This is a debated point between the two interpretations about the need for external points to be added to happiness. It is an argument for the inclusive nature of happiness in a way that happiness includes a sufficient amount of external goods. And here is the reply given by those who understand happiness as one single good, not an inclusive good. When Aristotle brings other goods into his inquiry about happiness his point is not that these goods are intrinsic goods, but that these goods have a contribution to the virtuous activity of the soul. Between the goods of friends, wealth, and power and the virtuous activity there is a causal relation.

A happy person needs a sufficient amount of external goods. What is the meaning of "sufficient" here in relation with external goods? The answer to this question, in the light of *EN* I, is that a happy person needs as much of the external goods needed to perform virtuous acts. Because a happy person needs external goods as instruments of virtuous acts, the sufficient amount will be the amount necessary to perform these fine acts.

Thus, the possibility of virtuous activity is the measure for the amount of external goods needed.

The summary answers to the question 2. When someone is not born in a good family, or does not have good children, or is ugly, finds himself in the situation of not being able to do fine things, his/her ability to act virtuously is diminished. These are a disadvantage for anyone in that situation. Such a person does not have the equipment to perform fine acts. Thus, the self-sufficiency of happiness is not in tension with the need for the external goods to be added to it.

Happiness as the virtuous activity of the soul is achieved through individual effort. Such an effort needs external goods to be sustained over the course of a lifetime. These resources are decreased or even destroyed in times of misfortune. When we lose our friends, our wealth, and our power, our ability to perform virtuous acts is diminished. If this loss is severe and frequent, we can end up in the situation of no longer living well. In this way our happiness depends on our external goods.

The degree of loss and misfortune varies from case to case. This degree has an impact upon happiness. Happiness will increase or will decrease depending on how the level of virtuous activity is. It can reach a very low point when the destruction of our external goods is very severe, and thus, the virtuous activity is severely diminished. In a situation like that we can no longer be called happy. In this way, misfortune, by the destruction of the external goods, affects happiness indirectly, because it interferes with virtuous activity.

When a friend or child dies, the person who suffers the loss cannot perform virtuous acts. The pain brought by the loss is an impediment for fine activities. When someone does not have children or friends, that person lacks the equipment to do fine acts, but when someone had good friends and good children and they died, the pain and suffering of the loss will incapacitate that person to perform noble activities.

When someone loses his/her friends the loss is double. Friends are a resource to accomplish various virtuous ends, and their loss diminishes the resources to achieve virtuous activities. When a friend dies, the pain and the mourning of the remaining friends will impede them to perform virtuous activities. The suffering of the loss of a friend is an interference in the life of a person who wills to do noble actions. Thus, happiness is the virtuous activity of the soul and the external goods are not components of it, but they are the necessary equipment to perform it.

A happy person, because of loss and destruction of his/her external goods will be distressed but will not be miserable. Misery is the opposite of happiness. A happy person is a person who practices virtues and will never practice what is opposite to virtues. Such a person, with major and frequent loses, will not be in the worst possible situation a person can be.

If happiness is the virtuous activity of the soul, then misery or unhappiness, its opposite, is the lack of the virtuous activity of the soul. A miserable person is a person who lacks any virtuous activity. An unhappy person is an un-virtuous person. That is the reason for which the happy person will never do things that are vicious and base. Happiness consists in virtuous activity, and the external goods are resources for the ultimate end and not its constituents.

3.3 INCLUSIVISM

In this section I will present the contributions brought by the inclusivist scholars to the ongoing research about the meaning of relationship between happiness and external goods in *EN*. Their interests are varied, and I will focus mainly on their ways of posing the problem and then specifically on their contribution to the debate. The inclusivist scholars argue that the external goods are part of happiness, are presented in historical order. I will start by (1) giving a concise summary of how the inclusive interpretation understands happiness as an inclusivist good, and then, (2) I will present the five representative scholars. After this presentation, I will (3) put together a summary of the interpretative inclusivist strategy, and that will constitute my overall summary of this approach and it will be an interlocutor further on in this project.

3.3.1 Happiness as an Inclusive Good

The understanding of happiness as a composite good is explained as follows. Aristotle says that happiness is the ultimate unifying end for the sake of which humans perform all their good actions.[32] When some actions are done for the sake of happiness, the phrase "for the sake of" is understood in "constituent" terms. These good actions, which are ends in themselves, are

---

32. Annas, "Aristotle on Virtue and Happiness," 36.

"constituent" to happiness.[33] As an analogy, a cup of coffee is a good item for so many of us. But this good item is a composite good. The constitutive items of it are water, coffee extract, temperature, pressure, and for some, sugar. When all these are combined together in various ways and proportions, we obtain a desired, a good item: the cup of coffee.

The good actions performed by humans are worth doing and they all together are the content of the best and most desired kind of life, happiness.[34] This composite understanding of happiness offers a particular explanation of the finality and self-sufficiency of happiness. Because happiness "includes" in itself good and desirable actions it is final and self-sufficient. The best there is, it is included in itself; that is why, it is final and self-sufficient.[35] Because of this inclusion of all ends,[36] happiness is sought for its own sake, and not for the sake of something else.[37] This is how happiness is the ultimate aim of the science of Politics. In this architectonic structure of the ultimate political end, all other ends are "embraced" (*EN* I.2, 1094b6–7).[38] In a city, the ends of the sciences and of various parts of government are all constituent elements of the good of the state. The science of education will have its end of educated, mature people do their part for the good of the state. The economy, the army, and all other endeavors will have their ends as constitutive the ultimate good of the state.

3.3.2 J. Cooper

According to Cooper, Aristotle understands the "human flourishing" based on several factors: complete life, practice of human virtues, and sufficient external goods.[39] In the Hellenistic times, according to Cooper, *EN* was treated as an "authoritative text" when someone was looking for the Aristotelian position concerning the human good.[40] The goods needed by people

---

33. Ackrill, "Aristotle on *Eudaimonia*," 72; Irwin, "Permanent Happiness," 10.
34. Ackrill, "Aristotle on *Eudaimonia*," 63; Pakaluk, *Aristotle's Nicomachean Ethics*, 319.
35. Gomez-Lobo, "Ergon Inference," 183.
36. Höffe, *Aristotle*, 151.
37. Ackrill, "Aristotle on *Eudaimonia*," 65.
38. Ackrill, "Aristotle on *Eudaimonia*," 68; Urmson, *Aristotle's Ethics*, 119; Hester, "Aristotle on the Function of Man," 12.
39. Cooper, "Aristotle on the Goods of Fortune," 174.
40. Cooper, "Aristotle on the Goods of Fortune," 176.

are understood in a broader way and they include the goods of the body and the external goods of wealth, power, and friends.[41] But according to Cooper, the relationship between these goods and the human person has to be defined as exactly as possible: the external goods are the external products of our virtuous actions. When someone rightly achieves a particular possession, that possession, that is other than knowledge or virtue, will be an external good.[42]

When the external goods are destroyed or lost, "one's blessedness [is] disfigured."[43] This is so, because εὐδαιμονία needs a sufficient supply of goods for performing virtuous activities. Cooper acknowledges that this reason for the needs of external goods in the life of the virtuous and happy person is difficult to explain, but he understands it as pointing to how the virtuous actions are hindered if this person does not have them.[44] This explanation is obscure and in need for further clarification. Cooper offers the explanation as follows:

> One central context for the exercise of the virtues is in the raising of children and the subsequent common life one spends with them, once adult, in the morally productive common pursuit of morally significant ends. If this context is not realized in one's life then, Aristotle would be saying, one's virtuous activities are diminished and restricted.[45]

This is how, according to Cooper, Aristotle distinguishes between the instrumentality of the external goods and the contexts that are created by the existence of the external goods.[46] Thus, when someone has them, s/he can do a variety of virtuous activities, and when s/he does not have them his/her blessedness is marred.

Cooper considers that the external goods in Aristotle have to be seen as "goods of fortune" because someone either has them or not and that is dependent on luck. No one has control over them. But the "goods of fortune" contribute to happiness of a person when this person reaps the effects these goods have on his/her future activities.[47]

41. Cooper, "Aristotle on the Goods of Fortune," 177.
42. Cooper, "Aristotle on the Goods of Fortune," 178.
43. Cooper, "Aristotle on the Goods of Fortune," 180.
44. Cooper, "Aristotle on the Goods of Fortune," 182.
45. Cooper, "Aristotle on the Goods of Fortune," 183.
46. Cooper, "Aristotle on the Goods of Fortune," 184.
47. Cooper, "Aristotle on the Goods of Fortune," 184.

This understanding of the role of the external goods is found, Cooper says, in the peripatetic tradition of Arius Didymus (beginning of first century AD), Aspasius (second century AD), and Alexander of Aphrodisias (second century AD).[48] All these ancient authors, according to Cooper, confirm that Aristotle requires the "external goods as one element in *eudaimonia*." A virtuous person knows the good use of any external goods in any circumstance (even in adversity). These peripatetic authors understand the role of the external goods in the same way. Virtues equip people to act morally in a wide variety of situations,[49] and will use whatever the external goods have at his/her disposal to the best possible. This is what the virtues essentially are: how the external goods are best used in any circumstance.[50]

Thus, according to Cooper, the external goods are integrated in *eudaimonia*, and this means that their value is seen in how they contribute to the performed virtuous activity.[51] This insight is based on Aristotle's thought that the character of a human being is determined by what that person does.[52] So, according to Cooper, Aristotle goes beyond the role of instrumentality for the external goods in the life of the virtuous person, to that of them being "a second component of *eudaimonia*, alongside virtuous activity." This integrative understanding of the external goods as a component of εὐδαιμονία is based, according to Cooper, on the effect the external goods have upon how the virtuous human being continues to live his/her virtuous life.[53]

3.3.3 T. Irwin

According to Irwin, Aristotle's definition as activity of the soul expressing complete virtue is subject to fortune. The reason for this is that, to acquire and actualize virtue, goods of fortune are needed.[54] Irwin interprets the major texts from *EN* I.8 about the relationships between happiness and external goods as pointing in two directions: the external goods are either

---

48. Cooper, "Aristotle on the Goods of Fortune," 185.
49. Cooper, "Aristotle on the Goods of Fortune," 187.
50. Cooper, "Aristotle on the Goods of Fortune," 188.
51. Cooper, "Aristotle on the Goods of Fortune," 188.
52. Cooper, "Aristotle on the Goods of Fortune," 195.
53. Cooper, "Aristotle on the Goods of Fortune," 196.
54. Irwin, "Permanent Happiness," 5.

(a) instruments for virtuous action, or (b) contributors to happiness apart from (a).[55]

There is a sense in which, according to Irwin, all external goods are "resources" used properly by a virtuous person, but not all the external goods are goods because they are used by someone virtuous. Irwin explores this non-instrumental type of external goods by mentioning Aristotle's text from *EN* I.8, 1099b2–6 where low-birth, solitude, being childless makes someone a poor candidate for happiness. The reason for this, according to Irwin, is not the pain, frustration or impediment produced by the loss or the absence of these goods, but the fact that these goods are goods valued for their own sake, and when they are lost or absent, happiness is not possible.[56]

Every one of these external goods are part of happiness, because they are related to virtue. That is why, according to Irwin, a vicious person has no part of happiness at all. Such a person will use badly these goods. The use of these external goods is what makes them to be part of happiness.[57]

Examining the role of fortune (good and bad) Irwin says that when external goods are acquired or lost, they have an effect upon happiness. When external goods are acquired, they make someone who is happy to be happier, and when the external goods are lost, they deprive that person of his happiness, but not to the point of making him unhappy.[58]

Irwin says that the key to understand these alternatives is found in how Aristotle explains completeness. Someone is happy, Irwin says, if his/her virtues and external conditions allow him/her to fulfill various capacities in right order and proportion.[59] This fulfillment of various capacities with the help of virtue and external conditions does not produce a greater good than happiness already possessed. Good fortune does not give anyone a greater good than happiness. When the external goods are lost or absent, because they are a part of happiness, happiness decreases. Irwin introduces an important distinction between virtue as a crucial part of happiness and external goods as part of happiness. Virtue as a crucial part of happiness is

---

55. Irwin, "Permanent Happiness," 6.
56. Irwin, "Permanent Happiness," 6.
57. Irwin, "Permanent Happiness," 6.
58. Irwin, "Permanent Happiness," 7.
59. Irwin, "Permanent Happiness," 8–9.

always retained, and the external goods, being goods of fortune, can be lost, and their loss have an impact upon happiness.[60]

3.3.4 M. Nussbaum

Nussbaum's approach on the relationship between εὐδαιμονία and external goods focuses on "activity and disaster."[61] Nussbaum identifies the particularities of Aristotle's choice of speaking about εὐδαιμονία as "an activity," as *Metaphysics* IX tells us, and the destructive power of disaster and how εὐδαιμονία is able to survive even the worst of them. That is why, this position is labeled "proto-stoic," which means that not even the worst events have the ability to affect the virtuous person, and this "stoic" position, Nussbaum says, was uphold by Aristotle long before the stoics. Thus, Nussbaum, in the light of *Met* IX, understands εὐδαιμονία as "activity/*energeia*" to mean that "*energeiai* are activities that are complete at any moment. They have their form in themselves."[62] This metaphysical understanding of εὐδαιμονία as an activity is fundamental for Nussbaum when she asks: "Is *eudaimonia* vulnerable? How far can it resist against disaster?"[63]

According to Nussbaum, Aristotle mentions two ways of understanding the relationship between good life and chance. (1) The good life is about "activities that are maximally stable and invulnerable to chance." (2) Good living and "actual activity according to excellence" are distinct, and based on this, when someone is in a virtuous condition, that is enough for εὐδαιμονία.[64] According to Nussbaum, Aristotle's argument is a combination of these two.[65] This combination is seen in the fact that εὐδαιμονία, on the one hand requires "actual activity" to reach its intended aim/end, and on the other hand, disaster can disrupt good activity. Every good action can be affected decisively by luck. Because there is a distinction between "being good" and "living well" when disaster strikes and the good life is gone, even the virtuous state/being good is impacted.[66] This state of "being good" is understood by Nussbaum as the condition at which someone

60. Irwin, "Permanent Happiness," 10.
61. Nussbaum, *Fragility of Goodness*, 318.
62. Nussbaum, *Fragility of Goodness*, 326.
63. Nussbaum, *Fragility of Goodness*, 318.
64. Nussbaum, *Fragility of Goodness*, 319–20.
65. Nussbaum, *Fragility of Goodness*, 322.
66. Nussbaum, *Fragility of Goodness*, 322.

arrives by moving from mere potentiality. "Being good" is the flourishing of someone's potentiality.[67]

But, this activity according to excellence operates properly in certain conditions, it needs resources, good health and a particular social context.[68] When someone is tortured "on the wheel" s/he cannot act justly. Εὐδαιμονία as an activity is vulnerable and it can be impeded. There are various ways in which actions that are beyond our control can interfere with εὐδαιμονία.[69]

A test case for εὐδαιμονία, as Aristotle understands it, is the story of king Priam (Aristotle mentions the misfortunes of king Priam in *EN* I.9, 1100a5–9). The loss of the Troy's war and the death of his sons did not destroy the quality of the king's life, because all the way to the end, king Priam showed good character through his actions,[70] even when Achille's son kills him. The virtues of character are stable dispositions and the dislodging of someone from these is a rare event, even when the conditions of the living well are destroyed. The good life can be taken away by disaster, but rarely the good character.[71] The damage done by disaster can be resisted by "good character and practical wisdom"; character and wisdom will help that person to continue to "act nobly."[72]

Nussbaum's conclusion is that "an Aristotelian conception of *eudaimonia*, which bases excellent activity on stable goodness of character, makes the good life tolerably stable in the face of the world."[73] This conclusion focuses the study of εὐδαιμονία as ἐνέργεια on virtues of character. The completeness of εὐδαιμονία as ἐνέργεια makes it hard to be dislodged.

3.3.6 D. Russell

Russell, as an inclusivist interpreter, understands happiness in *EN* as being summarized in *EN* I.10, 1101a14–16: happiness cannot consist in virtuous activity alone because this would leave out important goods for human life (beauty, strength, social position). The implication is that virtue alone is

---

67. Nussbaum, *Fragility of Goodness*, 324.
68. Nussbaum, *Fragility of Goodness*, 325; Broadie, *Ethics with Aristotle*, 54.
69. Nussbaum, *Fragility of Goodness*, 327.
70. Nussbaum, *Fragility of Goodness*, 329.
71. Nussbaum, *Fragility of Goodness*, 329.
72. Nussbaum, *Fragility of Goodness*, 333.
73. Nussbaum, *Fragility of Goodness*, 334.

not sufficient for happiness.[74] Russell sees virtue and external goods as they relate to happiness in two different ways: (1) virtue is the controlling factor, and (2) the external goods are dependent factors. A human being in relation to happiness is both an agent and a patient. This is so because there are activities that we engage in, and there are things that are done to us.[75]

The external goods Aristotle says, according to Russell, have two roles in relation to happiness: (1) instruments for supporting and facilitating virtuous activity, and (2) they are desirable for their own sake. When these goods desirable for their own sake are lost, that loss prevents one to be happy.[76] The fact that virtue controls happiness, and fortune might prevent it, is a problem that needs to be solved by Aristotle. Thus, on the one hand, because virtue controls happiness, no happy man can become wretched, and on the other hand, because of the suffering inflicted by bad fortune, no one can call someone like Priam in his suffering to be happy, but not unhappy either. According to Russell, Aristotle did not offer a third alternative here; he acknowledged a problem without settling it.[77]

Russell argues that the problem Aristotle has to solve is a triad of theses in tension with each other: (1) the control of virtue upon happiness, (2) the external and bodily goods are part of happiness, and (3) these external and bodily goods are not activities or part of activities.[78] These three theses are explained by Russell as follows. (1) The control of virtue upon happiness means that: "whatever else we may need; it is primarily virtuous activity that defines the tenor of a life where happiness is concerned."[79] This control of virtuous activity is a reflection of our nature as rational agents. (2) But the fact that the external goods are part of happiness is a reflection of our nature as patients. Russell explains how the external goods are part of happiness in the following way: "they are as such that (for the virtuous, anyway) life is better with them than without them, for their own sake."[80] (3) When Aristotle explores virtuous activity and happiness, he, according to Russell, assumes an embodied view of the self. This is seen, according to Russell, in Aristotle's interpretation of friends as the greatest of the external

---

74. Russell, *Happiness for Humans*, 82.
75. Russell, *Happiness for Humans*, 91.
76. Russell, *Happiness for Humans*, 108.
77. Russell, *Happiness for Humans*, 109.
78. Russell, *Happiness for Humans*, 109.
79. Russell, *Happiness for Humans*, 112.
80. Russell, *Happiness for Humans*, 112.

goods (*EN* IX.8, 1169b8–10). "Friendship is not a good in addition to, or as a context for, virtuous activity, but is itself a kind of virtuous activity from which one's friend is inseparable." That is the reason for which when a friend dies those constitutive activities of one's life are forever lost, closing off the possibility of living that life any more.[81]

3.3.7 T. Roche

Roche approaches the relationship between happiness and external goods asking the following question: "What is the contribution of external goods to happiness?"[82] Roche interprets Aristotle as working with a revised definition of his earlier sketch of happiness. The initial definition from *EN* I.7 is revised in I.10 where external goods are now part of the understanding of happiness.[83]

Roche agrees with the inclusivist interpreters that the external goods make an intrinsic contribution to someone's happiness, but, he says, that an important qualification needs to be added. This qualification is this: "an external good, for Aristotle, can directly promote a person's happiness only if that person is a virtuous person and therefore pursues and uses external goods in an excellent manner." Thus, this intrinsic direct contribution to happiness is due to the agent who acts in accordance with virtue.[84]

For Roche the external goods make a direct contribution to happiness. The fact that the external goods need to be added to happiness is understood by Roche as meaning that happiness cannot exist for a person if that person does not have them.[85] Aristotle's main point in *EN* I.8, 1099a31–b8, according to Roche, is not how various people acquire virtue and happiness, but how already virtuous persons suffer the loss of happiness.[86] A similar point is made, according to Roche, in *EN* I.8, 1099b26–28, where Aristotle refers to external goods as necessary constituents, and when these goods are lost, happiness is eliminated.[87]

---

81. Russell, *Happiness for Humans*, 114.
82. Roche, "Happiness and External Goods," 35.
83. Roche, "Happiness and External Goods," 35.
84. Roche, "Happiness and External Goods," 40.
85. Roche, "Happiness and External Goods," 47.
86. Roche, "Happiness and External Goods," 51.
87. Roche, "Happiness and External Goods," 53.

3.3.7 The Inclusive Good and the External Goods

If happiness is a composite of intrinsic goods, the external goods are its constituents. If happiness is a comprehensive good, and the goods which are dependent on fortune are authentic, then happiness must include them. If the external goods have to be included in happiness, when they are added, they will cause a good which is better than the most complete good (which is impossible). This difficulty needs to be addressed and solved.

Happiness is defined by Aristotle as the activity of the soul expressing complete virtue. The external goods need to be added to it because virtue needs them to be actualized. For example, magnanimity cannot be expressed if someone is not rich, and our friends cannot be part of our lives if they died. The external goods have two roles in relation to happiness: (a) they are its instruments to perform fine actions, and (b) when they are lost, they mar blessedness. The external goods are integrated in happiness, and this means that their value is seen in how they contribute to the performed virtuous activity. This insight is based on Aristotle's thought that the character of a human being is determined by what a person does.

So, Aristotle goes beyond the role of instrumentality for the external goods in the life of the virtuous person, to that of them being a second component of happiness, alongside virtuous activity. This integrative understanding of the external goods as a component of happiness is based on the effect the external goods have upon how the virtuous human being continues to live his/her virtuous life. Thus, for any of the external goods to be constituents of happiness, they need be related to virtue. For example, a vicious person who is wealthy, powerful, and handsome will not be happy because he misuses these goods (*EN* V.1, 1129b1–4).

Because virtuous activities control happiness, it cannot be taken away easily. When the external goods are taken away, it is not the same with our integrity which is retained. Such a person will never do despicable things; thus, s/he will not become miserable (*EN* I.10, 1100b23–35).

When the external goods are gained or when they are lost the following two things happen: when the external goods increase, they make the person happier, and when they are lost, they deprive that person of happiness, but that event does not make that person unhappy. There is a distinction between good living and virtuous activity, and based on this distinction, when someone is in a virtuous condition, that is enough for happiness.

The first situation is difficult to explain because it seems to conflict with what Aristotle says about happiness as being complete. If external goods are added and this make a person happier, then the complete good can become a better good, which means it was not complete in the first place if it needs external goods to be added. The gain or the loss of the external goods affect someone's happiness without making the person no longer happy. Because there is a distinction between being good and living well, when disaster strikes and the good life is gone, the virtuous state/being good is impacted, but not gone.

Such claims need to be explained based on how Aristotle understands completeness. The goods which are constituents of happiness are determinable. A determinable good is a good which helps the virtuous person to perform noble actions. When s/he does these actions, s/he is very pleased, and s/he treasures them greatly. Thus, these goods make him/her happier, but they do not produce a greater good than the happiness s/he already had.

When the good fortune happens, it makes him/her happier, but it does not give him/her a greater or more complete good than the happiness s/he already had. When the bad fortune happens, the effects are more serious. The reason for this is that, the happy life requires a moderate level of external goods. Because of bad fortune, these external goods are lost, and the person is no longer happy; but s/he does not become unhappy.

Thus, these are the determinable parts of happiness. When a person has all of them, s/he is happy, but when one of them is lost, that person is not happy. Nonetheless, there is a difference between losing all of these parts and having only some of them. A virtuous person will always have the crucial part of happiness without which all the external goods are not part of happiness at all. This is the difference between a virtuous and a non-virtuous person: a virtuous person will always have a part of happiness, but the non-virtuous person will have no part of happiness regardless of how many external goods has.

For Aristotle virtue is the dominant part of happiness. Virtue always comes first when Aristotle talks about happiness. No other good or combinations of goods has precedence over virtue in relation to happiness. Virtue, as the dominant component of happiness is not likely to fail because of bad fortune. For as long as it is stable, happiness is continuous. The fact that virtuous activity controls happiness does not mean that the virtuous activity is sufficient for it, or that happiness consists only in virtuous activity or any other of their consequences. What Aristotle says is that virtuous activity, in the right circumstances, will have a decisive role in relation to happiness. A circumstance is right when the external goods are present, and the person is virtuous and perform fine acts.

When a person adapts to the changes of fortune, we should be suspicious because the stable virtuous character is not there. Such a person does not choose the dominant part of happiness, which is virtue, but the other lesser goods. Such a choice is pointless because without the dominant part of virtue, happiness is not possible. Such a person, because of his/her choice, shows that does not know what happiness and virtue are. But continuity is related to virtue as the dominant, stable component of happiness. Virtue is not exposed to destruction by the bad fortune, that is why, it is continuous. Thus, happiness may not be continuous as it is affected by various fortunes, but virtue it is continuous.

Thus, happiness is not stable and thus is vulnerable to fortune and external factors. But fortune does not determine if someone is happy or not. We should not make ourselves adaptable to external circumstances. When someone is not flexible about the right things, his inflexible answer is right. Even though happiness is not stable, its dominant component, virtue, is. A virtuous person is committed to virtue and this fact is explained and justified by what the good is for a rational agent.

3.4 CONCLUSION

This is how the monistic interpretation of the ultimate good, happiness, explains the various questions in relation to the need for external goods to be added to it. Happiness is a self-sufficient good, so it does not need anything to be added to it *per se*; but because happiness is the virtuous activity of the soul, virtuous activity needs resources to be performed. So, the external goods are tools or resources of happiness.

The fact that happiness is controlled by virtue, and that virtuous activity requires resources to do fine acts, it needs external goods. The nature of virtue is seen in virtuous activities. There is not activity without resources. The amount of these resources depends on the kind of virtuous activity. The equipment with external goods is proportionate to the virtuous act that is performed.

The impact of fortune affects happiness because virtuous activity will no longer be possible. The external goods are lost or diminished. So, bad fortune will be an impediment to happiness. The loss of a good child or a friend constitutes both diminished resources and an impediment because of the deep pain caused by the loss. Even in this deep pain, a happy person will not be miserable. Misery is the opposite of happiness. Because of the dominance of virtue, the happy person will not be miserable, which means doing base or unvirtuous actions. His/her character is stable enough to not do vicious acts.

This is how the inclusivist interpretation of the ultimate good, happiness, explains the various questions in relation to the need for external goods to be added to it. Happiness is a self-sufficient good, so it does not need anything to be added to it *per se*; but because it is an inclusive good, various intrinsic goods are added to it. When these goods are added, it does not make the complete good better, but it does make the person happier. The external goods are constituents of happiness.

These goods are needed because through them the virtue is realized. They are another component of happiness alongside virtuous activity. When goods are lost, happiness is marred, but the person is not unhappy. There is a distinction between good living and virtuous activity. When disaster strikes good living is gone but being good is impacted but not gone. The external goods do not make happiness a more complete good, but they make the person happier. Virtue is not exposed to destruction by the bad fortune, but happiness is affected by it.

3.5 THIS PROJECT

Thus, this is the academic context in which I advance my thesis. It is a rich and complex context in which these two main positions are defended vigorously. The solution I propose acknowledges the external goods as *constituents* of happiness. So, it will be a refinement of the inclusivist interpretation. But it goes beyond it by bringing another type of dependency into play: the anthropological dependency.

In my understanding, the fact that Aristotle says that happiness needs external goods to be added to it can be explained by bringing together several premises. In this bringing together of these important factors stays the contribution of this thesis. Happiness has a multiple dependency upon external goods: (1) an instrumental dependency, (2) a constitutive dependency, and (3) an anthropological dependency.

(1) The instrumental dependency refers to the need for equipment to perform virtuous acts (*EN* I.8). This is a two-way street: on the one hand,

the external goods, such as friends, wealth, and political power, are resources for practicing virtue, and on the other, this practice of virtue, through them, leads to the transformation of the moral agent. This instrumental dependency is an indirect contribution of the external goods to happiness.

(2) The constitutive dependency refers to the fact that the external goods are constitutive to happiness based on how happiness is self-sufficient (*EN* I.8). The self-sufficiency of happiness is a relational political concept founded upon the self-sufficiency of the city. These relational political realities are part of happiness is, and when they are lost, happiness is a distant reality, or really lost. The impact of the loss is decisive in relation to happiness because of this constitutive dependency of happiness upon external goods. This constitutive dependency is a direct contribution of the external goods to happiness.

(3) The anthropological dependency refers to the fact that external goods are needed because we are human beings (*EN* X.8). The anthropological dependency does not refer to the previous two dependencies but is due to the fact that our human nature is not self-sufficient for contemplation, the perfect happiness. Health, food, and other arrangements are needed for us as human beings to be alive; only by being alive, we can experience happiness. This anthropological dependency is an indirect contribution of the external goods to happiness.

The argument of this project is organized in the following chapters. Chapter 4 is an analysis of the meaning of self-sufficiency of the ultimate end, happiness. Self-sufficiency of happiness is a major feature of happiness that answers the larger question if the definition provided by Aristotle to the ultimate end can accommodate the external goods or not. My answer is that it can. Then, the chapters 5, 6, and 7 are my analysis of the instrumental, constitutive, and anthropological dependencies. Chapter 8 is an analysis of the test of Priam and his losses. Chapter 9 is the conclusion of the project where I bring together my interpretation.

CHAPTER 4

THE POLITICAL SELF-SUFFICIENCY OF HAPPINESS

4.1 INTRODUCTION

THE MOST RECENT STUDIES on happiness and external goods no longer include a detailed analysis of the self-sufficiency of happiness. This is the case with the most recent work of Roche, Cashen, and Brown.[1] There are exceptions—like Russell and Cooper[2]—but there is no longer a direct connection between these topics, but mainly a necessary aspect that needs to be covered when someone inquires the topic of happiness; Cooper's study is focused on self-sufficiency, and that of Russell is a historical study of happiness.

Nonetheless, I argue that the dependency of happiness upon the external goods is better understood if self-sufficiency of happiness is integrated in the inquiry. The amount of work done on this topic is vast, and I will summarize it as it was unfolded in the larger debate between monism and inclusivism. My argument will be that the ultimate end of man is political in nature, being the end of the ruling science of politics, and its self-sufficiency has to be understood in political relational terms. This political

---

1. See Roche, "Happiness and External Goods"; Cashen, "Ugly, the Lonely, and the Lowly"; Brown, "Wishing for Fortune."
2. See Russell, *Happiness for Humans*; Cooper, *Knowledge, Nature, and the Good*.

perspective is founded on the political nature of humanity and on the self-sufficiency of the city. Happiness as the actualizing activity of the rational soul according to virtue is a political end, and its self-sufficiency depends on the self-sufficiency of the city. Only based on the self-sufficiency of the city, the ultimate political end is self-sufficient. This is how someone's life lacks in nothing and is worth choosing.

Thus, the structure of this chapter is organized as follows. (1) An overview of the debate concerning the meaning of self-sufficiency of happiness. This overview offers the scholarly context for my analysis. (2) My interpretation of happiness as the political end and as the activity of the soul according to virtue. Then, based on these insights, I will argue (3) that the self-sufficiency of happiness needs to be understood as a relational political concept. Happiness as the political end that embraces all intrinsic ends of life in the city is constituted of intrinsic relations which make it self-sufficient. This will be the foundation for my next points in the project where I will argue that the dependency of happiness on external goods is better explained as (a) enhancing dependency (chapter 5), (b) constitutive dependency (chapter 6), and (c) anthropological dependency (chapter 7).

4.2 THE MEANING OF SELF-SUFFICIENCY IN THE CURRENT DEBATES

This section presents a complex summary of how self-sufficiency of happiness was interpreted by the Aristotelian scholars. This summary of the debate will constitute my interlocutors when I will argue for my political understanding of the self-sufficiency of happiness later in the chapter. The textual data about self-sufficiency of happiness in *EN* is not extensive. The main text from *EN* I.7 is part of Aristotle's inquiry about the finality of happiness, and its self-sufficiency is a topic that is intended to strengthen the conclusion that happiness is final or complete:

> The same conclusion [that happiness is complete] also appears to follow from self-sufficiency. For the complete good seems to be self-sufficient. What we count as self-sufficient is not what suffices for a solitary person by himself,[3] living an isolated life, but what

---

3. This key phrase (τὸ δ᾽ αὔταρκες λέγομεν οὐκ αὐτῷ μόνῳ) is translated by other scholars as follows: "The term self-sufficient, however, we employ with reference not to oneself alone" (Rackham); "Now by self-sufficient we do not mean that which is sufficient for a man by himself" (Ross and Urmson); "By 'self-sufficient,' we do not mean sufficient for

suffices also for parents, children, wife, and, in general, for friends and fellow citizens, since a human being is a naturally political [animal].... Anyhow, we regard something as self-sufficient when all by itself it makes a life choiceworthy and lacking in nothing[4]; and that is what we think happiness does. (*EN* I.7, 1097b8–16, Irwin)

For Aristotle, the finality of happiness can be explained based on its self-sufficiency. The point he wants to make is that happiness, by itself, makes someone's life worth choosing and lacking in nothing.[5] Aristotle understands the term "self-sufficient" within his perspective of political anthropology. For him, a "a human being is by nature political" (φύσει πολιτικὸν ὁ ἄνθρωπος, *EN* I.7, 1097b10, Reeve).[6]

The meaning of self-sufficiency of happiness in *EN* I.7 is interpreted in two main ways by scholars: (1) for the scholars who understand happiness as the inclusive, ultimate good, its self-sufficiency means that it has all the necessary goods, and this makes life most desirable, and (2) for the scholars who understand happiness as the intellectual, ultimate good, its self-sufficiency means that happiness alone is enough to make life most

---

oneself alone" (Rowe); "We do not mean by self-sufficient what suffices for someone by himself" (Bartlett and Collins); "By 'self-sufficient,' however, we mean not self-sufficient for someone who is alone" (Reeve).

4. This key phrase (τὸ δ᾽ αὔραρκες τίθεμεν ὃ μονούμενον αἱρετὸν ποιεῖ τὸν βίον καὶ μηδενὸς ἐνδεᾶ) is translated by other scholars as follows: "We take a self-sufficient thing to mean a thing which merely standing by itself alone renders life desirable and lacking in nothing" (Rackham); "The self-sufficient we now define as that which when isolated makes life desirable and lacking in nothing" (Ross and Urmson); "The 'self-sufficient' we posit as being what in isolation makes life desirable and lacking in nothing" (Rowe); "As for the self-sufficient, we posit it as that which by itself makes life choiceworthy and in need of nothing" (Bartlett and Collins); "In any case, we posit that what is self-sufficient is what, on its own, makes a life choiceworthy and lacking in nothing" (Reeve).

5. Broadie says that self-sufficiency is applied by Aristotle to someone living among others (family, city), because every human being by his nature is social. When someone is happy, that person as a social being does not need anything more. See Broadie, *Ethics with Aristotle*, 32.

6. Joachim says that "we mean, therefore, an end sufficient by itself to satisfy man, who is by nature a social being and whose desires therefore extend to the wellbeing of his family, friends, and fellow citizens" (Joachim, *Aristotle*, 47). Sabou, too, says that "the lacking in nothing of happiness has to be understood in the context of its self-sufficiency, that is, in its political context" (Sabou, *Happiness as Actuality*, 78).

desirable than any other good.⁷ In the following two sections I present these two interpretations of self-sufficiency of happiness.

4.2.1 The Self-Sufficiency of the Inclusive Good

The inclusive interpretation of happiness understands the self-sufficiency of happiness as meaning that happiness is constituted of all intrinsic goods, and that makes life most desirable. For happiness to be self-sufficient it needs the set that embraces all goods; nothing is lacked. Happiness needs to include all goods to meet the criterion of self-sufficiency. Happiness is complete, and in this context of completeness, its self-sufficiency means that "all by itself" makes life lacking in nothing and worth choosing.⁸

Happiness is self-sufficient because it can provide all that is necessary for someone's parents, children, wife, friends and fellow citizens. Every human being is social, so taking care of others is part of what we are. This fact of self-sufficiency makes life desirable and not wanting anything.⁹ Self-sufficiency of the good life means that it lacks in nothing. Nothing that is added to it would make it more desirable. Friends make a life self-sufficient. That is why, self-sufficiency is relational. For humans, self-sufficiency is a life together with others.¹⁰ Self-sufficiency is an essential quality of a state.¹¹

A person is self-sufficient when s/he does not need anything. Because a human person is by nature political, a good human person will need good friends to fulfill his political nature. A good human person for being self-sufficient needs virtuous friends.¹² Happiness for us, humans, makes a social being want nothing more out of life.¹³

---

7. See also Curzer, "Criteria for Happiness," 423; *Aristotle & Virtues*, 409.
8. Irwin, "Conceptions of Happiness," 514.
9. Aquinas, *Commentary*.
10. See also the point made by Fossheim about aging as a fact of life: "The idea of self-sufficiency is something which is threatened by extreme old age. This is the time when one can no longer take care of one's family, one's business or economic welfare, or, ultimately, oneself. . . . Old age is when self-sufficiency can no longer be thought of in any way in terms of the single individual" (Fossheim, "Happiness and Old Age"). See also Sherman, *Fabric of Character*, 128; Shields, *Aristotle*, 396; Anagnostopoulos, *Aristotle on the Goals*, 291.
11. Anagnostopoulos, *Aristotle on the Goals*, 291.
12. Apostle, *Aristotle*, 337, 339.
13. Broadie, *Ethics with Aristotle*, 32.

4.2.2 The Self-sufficiency of the Intellectual Good

The intellectual interpretation of happiness understands the meaning of self-sufficiency of happiness as meaning that happiness alone is sufficient to make life desirable. Happiness is sufficient by itself as the most final end. It does not need anything else to make a life lacking in nothing and being most choiceworthy. Thus, if something is the final end, it is self-sufficient.[14] The human good is self-sufficient, which means that this good is sufficient to make life desirable and lacking in nothing.[15] The self-sufficiency of happiness is an activity which by itself, and without anything else, makes life choice-worthy and complete.[16]

Aristotle adds the need for external goods for a self-sufficient good. This means, according to the monistic interpretation, that happiness as the self-sufficient good does not include the most important goods and other goods needed for living in the city. The criterion of self-sufficiency helps us to determine the aim of the happy life; it is not intended to reiterate how many good things are found in the happy life.[17] Self-sufficiency is a mark of the ultimate aim of action. Being self-sufficient is the evidence of being most final.[18] A good is self-sufficient when all things we are committed to as desirable are choiceworthy for the sake of that good. The self-sufficiency of happiness is the self-sufficiency it has of itself to be the ultimate aim of a network of pursuits that is worth choosing.[19]

This debate about the meaning of self-sufficiency of happiness in *EN*, comes down to how do we need to understand the completeness of happiness: (1) the completeness as referring to a good that embraces all intrinsic goods and that makes it self-sufficient, because it has everything by itself, or (2) completeness as perfection referring to a single ultimate good that,

---

14. See also Almeida's analysis of Richardson Lear position when he says that for her: "Self-sufficiency is a function of the normative aspect of the finality of *eudaimonia*" (Almeida, "Gabriel Richardson Lear").

15. Richardson Lear, *Happy Lives*, 47–48; "Happiness," 397; See also Stone, who says that "for Aristotle the first two expressions 'self-sufficient' and 'complete,' both refer to the same property of the good. Aristotle defines both of them in terms of being desirable" (Stone, "Interpretation of Aristotle's Notion of Happiness," 82).

16. Kenny, "Happiness," 101; Heinaman, "*Eudaimonia* and Self-Sufficiency," 47.

17. Richardson Lear, *Happy Lives*, 48, 51.

18. Richardson Lear, *Happy Lives*, 52; "Happiness," 397.

19. Richardson Lear, *Happy Lives*, 59, 63.

on its own, makes life choiceworthy. I will analyze this debated issue and propose a way forward in the next section.

4.3 COMPLETENESS OR PERFECTION?

The debated phrase is from *EN* I.7, 1097b8: τὸ τέλειον ἀγαθόν/the final good/the complete good. The older translations of Ross and Rackham prefer final good, and newer translations of Urmson, Irwin, Bartlett and Collins, Crisp, and Reeve prefer complete good. The Greek term τέλειος means both complete and final.[20] So, the meaning of this key term needs to be discerned based on the context in which it is used.

The meaning of teleology in *EN* I is the factor that can help with the interpretation of this key phrase. Aristotle has an extensive usage of τέλος in *EN*.[21] I identify three major components of this usage: (1) the overall philosophical aspect according to which τέλος is "the Good at which all things aim" (*EN* I.1, 1094a18), (2) the overall political aspect according to which τέλος as "the Good of man must be the end of the science of Politics" (*EN* I.1, 1094b6), and (3) the overall perspective in which "virtue ensures the rightness of the end aimed at, [and] prudence ensures the rightness of the means we adopt to gain that end" (*EN* VI.12, 1144a32). These aspects of philosophy, politics, and virtues need to be in view when teleology is explored in *EN*.

The immediate context from *EN* I.7 points towards the political aspect as the component important for interpretation. Aristotle says that, the complete/final good seems to be self-sufficient, and explains self-sufficiency in a larger relational circle, from parents to fellow citizens. Based on this political context, I argue that for a well-grounded interpretation of what the phrase "final/complete good" means, it is needed to explore the meaning of completeness/perfection in political terms as happiness is the end of the science of politics, and then a case for the political self-sufficiency can be made. This is what I will do in the next sections.

---

20. Liddell et al., *Greek-English Lexicon*, 1770.

21. *EN* 1094a18; 1094b6; 1095a5; 1095b23, 31; 1097a21, 23; 1097b21; 1098b19; 1099b17, 30; 1100a11, 32; 1101a18; 1110a13; 1111b27; 1112b15, 34; 1113b4; 1114b1, 14, 16, 18, 24; 1115b13, 22; 1117b1, 3; 1139b2–3; 1140a29; 1140b6, 7; 1141b12; 1142b29–31, 33; 1143a9; 1143b10; 1144a32; 1145a5–6; 1152b23; 1153a9–11; 1174b33; 1176a31; 1176b28, 31, 35; 1179a34; 1179b1; cf. *TLG Workplace 7.0*.

4.3.1 The End of the Science of Politics

In this subsection I will present the scholarly context provided by the work of Hardie, van Cleemput, and Collins[22] in which it is studied the political aspect of Aristotle understanding of the ultimate end of humans.[23] Then, I will argue that the good of the individual, the complete good, is understood by Aristotle as being part of the good of the state. The highest good corresponds to the highest type of community, the city state. This status of being the highest type of community is given by its self-sufficiency.

The scholarly debate on εὐδαιμονία as the end of the political science in *EN* is mainly analyzed at the point of discerning what kind of end εὐδαιμονία is inclusive or monistic. For example, Hardie perceives Aristotle as "fumbling" for the inclusive understanding of τέλος because the end of politics embraces other ends[24]; but in the end, Hardie interprets εὐδαιμονία as a dominant end, recognizing the fact that Aristotle is ambiguous in his conception of the final good.[25]

What I do is that, I study the political aspect of the ultimate good for seeing if it is a complete or a perfect good. In this case, an important question is how and why Aristotle brings politics into his inquiry? What is the common ground between *EN* and politics? This is how various scholars bring life in the city/πόλις into their interpretation of εὐδαιμονία. For Hardie, the Aristotelian definition of what is peculiar to man is the active life of the element of the soul that has a rational principle (*EN* I.7, 1098a3–4) and this action can be understood to include contemplative thinking, as in *Politics* VII.3.[26] This is the common ground seen by Hardie between *EN* and *Politics*. This is a pioneering point, and it will be explored further by Van Cleemput (1999), and Collins (2004). *EN* and *Politics* are part of the larger Aristotelian teleological vision, as I will show this later in this subsection, but Hardie does not expand on this insight.

---

22. Hardie, "Final Good in Aristotle's Ethics"; Van Cleemput, "Aristotle on Happiness"; Collins, "Moral Virtue."

23. The scholarly literature on εὐδαιμονία as the end of the science of politics is growing. I mention here the most recent works I am aware of: Donoghue-Armstrong, "Teleology, Perfectionism, and Communitarianism," 118–66; Arnn, "Happiness and the Political Life."

24. Hardie, "Final Good in Aristotle's Ethics," 279.

25. Hardie, "Final Good in Aristotle's Ethics," 279.

26. Hardie, "Final Good in Aristotle's Ethics," 280.

Van Cleemput (1999) in his interpretation of εὐδαιμονία focuses his work on two major factors: man is a being that belongs in the city, and contemplation is perfect happiness.[27] These two constitute the larger framework for a political interpretation of εὐδαιμονία. According to Van Cleemput, the Aristotelian argument is not an argument that focuses primarily on the individual, but on the individual as a "political animal." That is why the Aristotelian interest is in the happiness of the πόλις.[28] Van Cleemput reaches the end of his argument by saying that in *Politics*, too, Aristotle sees contemplation as happiness. The philosophical and the political lives are not separate lives, but they come together into the ideal of the mixed life. The rulers of the πόλις are those that are capable of contemplation. The perfect happiness in the city is promoted through legislation that focuses on peace and leisure.[29] Thus, these two writings *EN* and *Politics*, because both of them focus on the topic of the highest human good, they have to be interpreted together.[30]

Van Cleemput brings the political element in the interpretation of εὐδαιμονία. Aristotle says that εὐδαιμονία is the final end of the ruling science (*EN* I.2). The question is, how are these two writings, *EN* and *Politics*, related? It is likely that *Politics*, in the form we have it, is an incomplete draft.[31] That is why, we do not take the work itself as something final but provisional. Thus, we have two writings (*EN* and *Politics*) from the same general science, the science of politics. Both of them have as their main theme the final end of man: εὐδαιμονία. I understand *EN* as the foundation for *Politics* not the other way around. *EN* is written with an eye on the *Politics* and informs it.

The foundational character of *EN*, as a political inquiry, is seen in its focus on the activities of the soul and transformation of character and attaining virtue. All of these are necessary for life in the city. But *Politics* can help us to unpack affirmations from *EN* where εὐδαιμονία is pictured in the larger context of the political science as it tries to ordain the life in the πόλις. The main subject of εὐδαιμονία is the final end of the political science, but in *EN* the focus is not so much on the legislation and the city work of the rulers, but on the εὐδαιμονία itself, on how should we understand it and

---

27. Van Cleemput, "Aristotle on Happiness," 2, 155.
28. Van Cleemput, "Aristotle on Happiness," 4.
29. Van Cleemput, "Aristotle on Happiness," 4.
30. Van Cleemput, "Aristotle on Happiness," 3.
31. Collins, "Ends of Action," 169; Ross, *Aristotle*, 248.

practice it at the personal level and in relationship with others. It is more an approach from the inside out, not the vice versa. Above all things, a true student of politics has to study ἀρετή and the facts about the soul (*EN* I.13), and *EN* offers an outline for this inquiry, and *Politics* offers an integration of εὐδαιμονία in the life of the πόλις and its varied challenges.

Collins takes this relationship between *EN* and *Politics* in the understanding of the human good and explores it further. She says that according to Aristotle, the political community and the law have an authoritative place in ordering human action.[32] For Collins, *EN* II–IV are examples of how the political power orders the education and virtue of the citizens of the πόλις. She, mainly, stays within the limits of *EN* to explore the meaning of εὐδαιμονία from a political point of view. *Politics* is brought into her analysis to show how Aristotle's vision from *EN* is reflected into it. Collins does not explain the relationship between *EN* and *Politics* but shows the common ground between them in the study of political science and its final end, the good of man. The weight of the law and the final human good find an expression in terms of justice: action toward the good of another. This is our full moral perfection and the completion of virtue.[33]

Even if Collins does not focus on the meaning of εὐδαιμονία as such (her focus is on political community and virtues), she brings to my attention the necessity of working out the implications of the fact that εὐδαιμονία is the final end of the ruling political science. "Action toward the good of another" brings together both the ethical and the political. It lacks the focus on the rational element of the soul, and it does not end with θεωρία, but it points to a social understanding of the good.

In this scholarly context, the finality of εὐδαιμονία in relation to political science needs to be explored further. My project is not in Aristotle's *Politics* but because for him the good of the individual and the good of the city are the same thing, I have to explore this common ground. This common identity of εὐδαιμονία both at individual and community level is differentiated by Aristotle when he says that the good of the city is greater and more complete than the good of the individual (*EN* I.2, 1094b10).

The good of an individual and the good of the city are the same thing, but the second is greater and more complete. Aristotle does not tell us why this difference exists, but I infer from his inquiry, that life in the city is seen as of greater value than the life of a single individual. Life in the city is a

---

32. Collins, "Moral Virtue," 48.
33. Collins, "Moral Virtue," 53.

sign of civilization, but life alone is not. To organize a society is of greater value than to live alone. In this way the good of the city is "greater and more complete" than the good of the individual. The difference is seen in terms of "satisfactory" and "finer and more divine" [ἀγαπητὸν/κάλλιον καὶ θειότερον] (*EN* I.2, 1094b12). This difference does not diminish the value of the individual but shows that there is something of greater value than being alone, and that is the good of the city. Most likely the reference to divinity is to be understood in the larger Aristotelian metaphysical framework. In that framework god is the pure actuality into which every potentiality reaches its destination. Life in the city is closer to achieving that actuality than the life of being alone. It is us, humans, achieving a more divine good. Humans are primarily political creatures, and the good of man is to be understood as having in view the good of a nation and cities [ἔθνει καὶ πόλεσιν] (*EN* I.2, 1094b10). In *Politics* I.1253a, he goes that far and says that the person who does not need to live in a city is either "a beast or a god," and by this he means that, that person is self-sufficient by himself.

This relationship between πόλις and ἀγαθός is to be explored with a view at *Politics* I. In *Politics* I, Aristotle shows the details of how his political inquiry into the meaning of εὐδαιμονία works out in his political system. The premises and their conclusion at the beginning of *Politics* I are like this:

(p1) mankind always acts in order to obtain that which they think good,

(p2) every community is established with a view to some good,

(p3) the state is the highest type of political community, and thus conclusion

(c) the state aims at the highest good (*Politics* I.1252a, Jowett).

In *Politics* I.1 there is the same teleological perspective as in *EN* I.1: "mankind always acts in order to obtain that which they think good." In *Politics* I, the activity of the humankind is that of establishing a πόλις which is done with some good in view. This is true about every city. The city and the political community (*Pol.* I.1252a) are the highest type of organization and embraces all the rest, and that is why, it aims at highest good. The highest good corresponds to the highest type of community, the city state.

The highest type status of the city is given by its self-sufficiency. The self-sufficiency of an entity is the result of being able to sustain itself. It depends on the ability, resources, and number. A family is more self-sufficient than an individual, and a city than a family (*Pol.* II.1261b). A city is established only when the community is large enough to be self-sufficient

(*Pol.* II.1261b). Thus, based on these political insights, I will argue in the next section that the self-sufficiency of εὐδαιμονία is a relational/political concept because it depends on the self-sufficiency of the πόλις.

4.4 POLITICAL SELF-SUFFICIENCY OF HAPPINESS

In this section I will engage first with the representative scholarship about the self-sufficiency of happiness in *EN* (Ackrill, Richardson Lear, Caesar), and then, I will present my argument exploring important concepts from *EN* I and *Politics* II about self-sufficiency. I will argue that the self-sufficiency of εὐδαιμονία depends upon the self-sufficiency of the city, thus it is a political concept. I will also present how this is relevant for exploring further the dependency of happiness upon external goods, such as political power, friends, and children.

Aristotle's inquiry on εὐδαιμονία as τέλος in *EN* I encompasses also the aspect of "self-sufficiency." The "self-sufficiency" aspect of εὐδαιμονία is a well-researched area and here is my engagement with it. Beginning with Ackrill there is the view that the self-sufficiency of εὐδαιμονία has to be understood in the larger debate about its nature as an inclusive or dominant end.[34] Ackrill argues for an inclusive understanding of εὐδαιμονία, and, based on this, self-sufficiency is mainly understood in negative terms as lacking in nothing.[35] Richardson Lear, who is on the monistic side of the debate, approaches the self-sufficiency of happiness by seeing it as a "plausible constraint."[36] By this she means that, when someone suffers a misfortune that person is essentially untroubled, because happiness is self-sufficient; the loss of external goods does not ruin happiness. But that person will no longer have the means to be generous towards others. Happiness is sufficient by itself to make a life worth choosing. In Richardson Lear's view, this is the reason for which the self-sufficiency of εὐδαιμονία does not imply inclusiveness.[37] The ultimate good is sufficient in itself for a worthy and attractive life. The self-sufficiency of the highest good depends on its being the end of the happy life.[38]

---

34. Ackrill, "Aristotle on *Eudaimonia*," 65–66.
35. Ackrill, "Aristotle on *Eudaimonia*," 66.
36. Richardson Lear, *Happy Lives*, 47.
37. Richardson Lear, *Happy Lives*, 48.
38. Richardson Lear, *Happy Lives*, 52.

I agree with Richardson Lear that the self-sufficiency of happiness is part of the teleological outlook of Aristotle; but my agreement with her stops there. I argue that in *EN* I.7 self-sufficiency is a positive political concept as it is in *Politics* II.1261b. The final good is self-sufficient because it is based on the self-sufficiency of the πόλις. The people as citizens of the political city have everything they need for a happy life. The stability of the εὐδαιμονία, when the bad events strike, is not so much based on its self-sufficiency, as the monistic interpretations says, but on a strong character which was forged through the practice of virtues. Happiness has everything someone needs for a happy life in the sense that it is grounded in the life of the self-sufficiency of πόλις where they have protection, laws, institutions, and resources for a good life.

Because Aristotle mentions "self-sufficiency" of εὐδαιμονία without too much introduction, there are scholars who see the reference to self-sufficiency in *EN* I.7 as "an abrupt recording" that cannot be interpreted on its own.[39] Caesar reads the meaning of self-sufficiency of εὐδαιμονία in the light of *EN* X.6. Caesar understands the self-sufficiency mainly in negative terms by saying that "happiness is *energeia* which is self-sufficient (lacks nothing)."[40] In my view this is a radical unnecessary reading because *EN* I.7 is the last major layer of Aristotle's inquiry into the finality of εὐδαιμονία. The inquiry is in the area of political science, and it is about the best life in the πόλις. The self-sufficiency is a positive concept (which can be, if necessary, expressed negatively as lacking in nothing). The city has the ability, resources and number to sustain itself. The political overview of Aristotle's inquiry has to be kept in view at all times.

I interpret Aristotle's saying about self-sufficiency of εὐδαιμονία by making reference to ideas expressed earlier in this chapter about the life in the city. Here, I start from the observation that Aristotle investigates about an end that is pursued in its own right (*EN* I.7, 1097a30); it is a final end and it is for its own sake, not for the sake of something else. What does it mean "in its own right"? This phrase leads in two directions: for what it is, and for its own sake. That means that the focus is on its inherent qualities, and on the implication of having certain qualities. We are dealing with an end in itself which is not an intermediary end towards something else. It stands by itself, that is, it does not need something else. This end is pursued because of what it is in itself.

---

39. Caesar, "Why We Should Not Be Unhappy," 219.
40. Caesar, "Why We Should Not Be Unhappy," 230.

THE POLITICAL SELF-SUFFICIENCY OF HAPPINESS

Aristotle's analysis of the "degrees of finality" [τελειότερον] (*EN* I.7, 1097a30) is important because it shows the dynamics of meaning brought into inquiry by the lexical choice of τέλος. The aspects of aiming and reaching an end, and of finality go together into the mix of ideas conveyed by Aristotle. Aristotle's argument is an "upward" one, going towards higher and higher levels. This means that it gets closer to god, the pure actuality in which all potentiality reaches its end. This is an end "more final in itself" [τέλειον τὸ καθ" αὑτό] (*EN* I.7, 1097a33) than any other one, it is an aim which is "absolutely final." Εὐδαιμονία is this type of τέλος because we choose it always for its own sake and not for the sake of something else (*EN* I.7, 1097b2).

Based on these observations, I explore the "self-sufficiency" aspect of εὐδαιμονία. The final good is a thing "sufficient in itself" (*EN* I.7, 1097b10). At this point Aristotle makes an important clarification that brings into his inquiry the political context for studying εὐδαιμονία. The self-sufficiency of the final good is not related to a life in isolation, but a life in society (*EN* I.7, 1097b15). This is so, because man is by nature political [φύσει πολιτικὸν ὁ ἄνθρωπος], a being that belongs to the πόλις. Self-sufficiency is a relational political concept. The highest type status of the city is given by its self-sufficiency. The self-sufficiency of an entity is the result of being able to sustain itself. It depends on the ability, resource and number. For example, as I mentioned earlier in the chapter, a family is more self-sufficient than an individual, and a city than a family (*Pol.* II.1261b). Thus, the self-sufficiency of εὐδαιμονία is a relational/political concept because it depends on the self-sufficiency of the πόλις.

These ideas developed in *Politics* II help me to explore the text from *EN* I.7. The ultimate/complete good is self-sufficient in someone's life when this person lives in the city with his/her family, friends, and fellow citizens. Because by nature the man is political, the self-sufficiency of the ultimate good of man has to be understood in political/relational terms. The ultimate good, the self-sufficiency, and the citizenship are the lines of Aristotle's inquiry at this point.

He does not speak about the self-sufficiency of someone who lives "a solitary life" [βίον μονώτην] who is "alone/solitary by himself" [αὐτῷ μόνῳ] (*EN* I.7, 1097b10). His/her existence is in the πόλις; s/he belongs in the city. The self-sufficiency of the ultimate good of men is based on the nature of man, which is a political nature. It is about life in a political community, in a city. Leaders, laws, institutions, family, friends, all are part in a political life. Self-sufficiency of happiness is based on the political nature of man. The self-sufficiency of εὐδαιμονία, the ultimate good/τέλειον ἀθαθὸν, can be attained only by living and being part in a city, because, by nature, every human is "a political thing" (*EN* I.7, 1097b11).

The structure of Aristotle's inquiry has these two premises: because

(p1) the political community/city is more self-sufficient than a family or an individual, and

(p2) man, by nature, is a political thing, it follows that conclusion

(c) the self-sufficiency of the ultimate good of man is politically based.

The self-sufficiency of happiness is thus identified and, Aristotle says, it makes life desirable and lacking in nothing.

The desirability and lacking in nothing define further the self-sufficiency of εὐδαιμονία. It has everything it needs, and it is the most desired of all good things. The "lacking in nothing" of εὐδαιμονία has to be understood in the context of its self-sufficiency, that is, in its political context. A city is more self-sufficient than a solitary man. "Lacking in nothing" does not mean that εὐδαιμονία is a static activity, because its completeness is understood as aiming and reaching the ultimate political good. It is a relational activity. In the city, the most self-sufficient entity available to humanity, every one of its citizens benefits from its self-sufficiency. It is not a perfect place, but the best available so far to every human being.

4.5 CONCLUSION

In this chapter I argued that an inquiry into the meaning of dependency of happiness upon external goods in *EN* needs an inquiry into the meaning of the self-sufficiency of happiness. I interpret the self-sufficiency of happiness in political terms. It means that the virtuous activity of the soul does not lack in anything and is worth choosing based on what the city can offer. The most self-sufficient entity available to man is a city, and man being a political creature, the city is the best place for him to live a life of happiness. Happiness as the final end of man is a political end. It is an end that is available to man in the city. Life in the city among the political leaders, friends, family has this feature of self-sufficiency. This is how the criterion of finality is also confirmed by the criterion of self-sufficiency, both are political in nature.

This intrinsic network of relations is what constitutes the good life, the life into which the political end is found. The political power, friends, and family are its constituents. That is why, when Aristotle mentions them as being needed to be added to happiness, describing them as external goods, they have to be seen also as constituents of the virtuous action of the rational soul. The dependency of happiness upon them is complex and, most likely, needs to be understood as (a) formative, (b) constitutive, and (c) anthropological. These three aspects of it will be explained and defended in the next three chapters.

CHAPTER 5

AN ENHANCING INSTRUMENTAL DEPENDENCY

5.1 INTRODUCTION

So far in this project I have argued that the self-sufficiency of happiness needs to be interpreted in political terms. Happiness is self-sufficient because its self-sufficiency is founded on the self-sufficiency of the city. Aristotle understands it in this way because he understands the nature of every human being in political terms. This political anthropology is the foundation for my interpretation of the dependency of happiness on external goods.

Based on this understanding of self-sufficiency as a political/relational concept, εὐδαιμονία as the virtuous activity of the soul has the external political power, goods of friends, good children, and beauty as constituents of it. In this chapter I will argue that the external goods have both an instrumental and a constitutive role in relation to εὐδαιμονία. In relation to their instrumental role, there is no debate, as every scholar agrees with it, but argues differently about it; Aristotle himself says that "it is impossible, or not easy, to perform fine actions if one is without resources. For in the first place many things are done by means of friends, or wealth, or political power, as if by means of tools" (*EN* I.8, 1099b1, Rowe).

The instrumentality of the external goods is a major factor for the possibility of εὐδαιμονία as actualizing virtuous activity. Thus, I will present a concise section on how the practice of virtue works, and what is its virtuous outcome. This is necessary because I interpret εὐδαιμονία as consisting in actualizing virtuous activity. The things/acts we do are the things we become. The noble acts are done with the help of external goods, and this doing is the key for reaching the actuality of our potentiality, our εὐδαιμονία. Thus, the instrumental aspect of the external goods is relevant to what εὐδαιμονία is. I will argue, in dialogue with the monistic interpreters,[1] that the instrumental status of the external goods is not simply external to happiness, but part of the process through which virtues are formed, and this process is actually a central aspect of εὐδαιμονία as the actualizing virtuous activity.

In relation to the constitutive role of the external goods, I will argue that they are part of εὐδαιμονία as actualizing virtuous activity. The self-sufficiency of the actualizing virtuous activity is a relational formative concept, and this centrality of relatedness makes the external goods of friends, good children, and beauty constituents of εὐδαιμονία. Aristotle explains their role as constituents of εὐδαιμονία by focusing on the circumstance of their loss. I will explore the impact of their loss and clarify the distinction between εὐδαιμονία and μᾶκᾶρία, because Aristotle never says that εὐδαιμονία is disfigured/maimed/ruined; instead he says these things about μᾶκᾶρία. Also, I will evaluate the tragic example of King Priam as a test case of extreme disaster and its impact upon happiness.

5.2 ISSUES AND SOLUTIONS

Aristotle explicitly says that the reason for which the external goods need to be added to happiness is the fact that "we cannot, or cannot easily, do fine actions if we lack the resources" (*EN* I.8, 1099a15, Irwin). The practice of virtue needs resources. Aristotle gives two different reasons for the need of external goods, one positive and one negative (γὰρ . . . δὲ).[2] (1) The posi-

---

1. I will interact with Kraut, *Aristotle on the Human Good*; Heinaman, "Eudaimonia and Self-Sufficiency"; Cashen, "Ugly, the Lonely, and the Lowly"; Brown, "Wishing for Fortune"; Roche, "Happiness and External Goods," as main representatives of the monistic interpretation and focus on their nuanced differences.

2. This phrase is translated in various ways: "first of all / further" (Irwin); "for / also" (Rackham); "for in the first place / and then again" (Rowe); "for / and" (Ross and Urmson); "for / again" (Crisp); "for / then again" (Reeve).

tive reason is given with the help of an analogy, that of instruments; as we use instruments to do various tasks, so we use friends, wealth, and political power to do many actions. (2) The negative reason is given to say what happens when we are deprived of certain externals: our blessedness is marred. These two reasons given by Aristotle are explained mainly in two ways by scholars. These two ways are based on how εὐδαιμονία is interpreted: either a monistic good or an inclusive good.

The monistic interpreters understand εὐδαιμονία as the single ultimate human good (virtuous activity alone), and they focus on the instrumentality of the external goods as their single role in relation to εὐδαιμονία. The role of the external goods in relation to happiness is seen as mainly causal.[3] For example, friends are at most instruments to the highest human good which is virtuous action.[4] When a virtuous person has enough external goods s/he can practice virtue, but when s/he is deprived of the external goods this is an impediment to virtuous activity.[5]

The monist interpreter will make sure that the goods necessary for happiness are not seen as similar with the happiness itself.[6] The external goods are conditions[7] for εὐδαιμονία, and when they are lost, the fact that they are gone, it hinders[8] εὐδαιμονία[9]; or they are seen as the equipment necessary to attain virtuous activity.[10] Thus, happiness is diminished[11]

---

3. See especially Kraut, who says that "happiness consists in virtuous activity alone, and the remaining goods bear some causal relation to this highest good" (Kraut, *Aristotle on the Human Good*, 259).

4. Richardson Lear, "Aristotle on Happiness," 131.

5. See also the recent debate between Roche and Cashen. Roche disagrees with Cashen about the extent of effect of this loss. Cashen interprets the loss of the external goods as having a devastating effect upon the moral development of the person who has lost the goods, and Roche says that Aristotle here refers to a mature person who already has a virtuous character and is eligible for political office (Roche, "Happiness and External Goods," 51).

6. Richardson Lear, "Happiness," 398.

7. Another analogy used by the monist interpreters is that of a cake: the external goods are not the ingredients used to make it, but the utensils required to do it (Scott, "Aristotle on the Good Life," 355).

8. Also, Curzer who says that "when the external goods are lost or absent, virtuous activity is hindered and happiness is detracted" (Curzer, *Aristotle & Virtues*, 419).

9. Heinaman, "*Eudaimonia* and Self-Sufficiency," 49.

10. Kraut, *Aristotle on the Human Good*, 260.

11. Also, Halim, who says that the loss of the external goods diminishes the range and magnitude of the virtuous action (Halim, "Aristotle's Explanation," 136).

indirectly by their loss.[12] The pain caused by the disaster and loss is felt deeply and this affects the ability to perform virtuous activity.[13] This indirect effect is the effect, the monistic interpreters are willing to accept. The singleness aspect of happiness as virtue activity alone is defended in this way. The effect of the disaster is not intrinsic, but only indirect.

The inclusivist interpreters disagree with the condition/equipment status of the external goods and argue for their component status. When these external goods are lost this is not just an impediment to virtuous activity, but their loss is a loss of happiness, because these goods are valued for their own sake, they are part of a total life.[14]

But still, there is some agreement, at least between Heinaman and Nussbaum, when Nussbaum interprets the externals as conditions necessary for action according to excellence.[15] Nonetheless, Nussbaum will go further and say that the externals are not just tools related to good activity, but that they are part of the specification of what a good action is.[16] A similar interpretation is given by Russell, another inclusivist scholar, who argues for both these two roles of the external goods, instrumental and constituent. Russell's point is that because the external goods are parts of happiness, life is better with them than without them.[17]

This disagreement between monistic and inclusivist interpreters can be approached, yet in another way. The instrumental role of the external goods is acknowledged by both of them, but, if I interpret εὐδαιμονία as actualizing virtuous activity, I can answer an important objection given by the monistic scholars[18] to the inclusivist scholars, namely that Aristotle understands εὐδαιμονία as gradual, existing in various degrees. The problem for the inclusivist scholars, the monist scholars say, is that when a person is happy, nothing can be added to that happiness; that good life cannot be increased, because happiness is a complete good.[19] But if εὐδαιμονία is interpreted as actualizing virtuous activity, I work with a dynamic concept

12. Kraut, *Aristotle on the Human Good*, 259.
13. Roche, "Happiness and External Goods," 50.
14. Irwin, "Permanent Happiness," 6.
15. Nussbaum, *Fragility of Goodness*, 325.
16. Nussbaum, *Fragility of Goodness*, 319.
17. Russell, *Happiness for Humans*, 109, 112.
18. See Heinaman, "Eudaimonia and Self-Sufficiency," 50.
19. See the classic debate between Heinaman and Irwin in Heinaman, "*Eudaimonia* and Self-Sufficiency," 49–50.

which is both a complete action in itself, and one that aims for reaching its perfect stage.

5.3 EXTERNAL GOODS AS INSTRUMENTS OF VIRTUE

The instrumentality of the external goods in relation to virtue needs to be clearly explained as its meaning can bring further understanding about its relationship to εὐδαιμονία. I will do that in this section by focusing on the nature of virtue and how it is formed. This will be the foundation to explain practice or action that is possible with the help of external goods. I will argue that the external goods are tools both for virtuous acts and for personal edification. Thus, I will explain that they are instruments both for personal virtue and public virtue. The three externals mentioned by Aristotle (friends, wealth, and political power) have to be interpreted together as they are tools for public good.

Virtue is mentioned for the first time in *EN* in I.5, 1095b29: "Virtue is a greater good than honor." Then, when compared with εὐδαιμονία, it does not pass the test of completeness to be the end of man; this is so because "it is possible to possess it while you are asleep" (*EN* I.5, 1095b32).[20] Also, excellence in all its forms is chosen for its own sake (*EN* I.7, 1097b3).[21] Aristotle examines the nature of virtue because virtue is part of his definition of εὐδαιμονία (*EN* I.13, 1102a5). As εὐδαιμονία, virtue too is related to the soul; εὐδαιμονία is an activity of the soul, and virtue is the excellence of the soul (*EN* I.13, 1102a16).

As the soul consists of two parts, one irrational (vegetative that causes nutrition and growth, and appetites and desire) and the other capable of reason (*EN* I.13, 1102a29), the virtue is differentiated in correspondence with this division of the soul: intellectual virtues such as wisdom, intelligence and prudence, and moral virtues such as liberality, and temperance (*EN* I.13, 1103a5–7). The intellectual virtues are produced and increased by instruction, and moral virtues are the product of habit (*EN* II.1, 1103a15–16). The moral virtues are not part of our nature, but our nature gives us the capacity to acquire them (*EN* II.1, 1103a25). We acquire virtues by practicing them; we become just by doing just acts (*EN* II.1, 1103b1). This

---

20. See also Annas, "Aristotle on Virtue and Happiness," 35.

21. Also, Annas who interprets Aristotle's position as saying: "to act virtuously is to do what is noble—what virtue requires—for its own sake and for no other reason" (Annas, "Aristotle on Virtue and Happiness," 40).

is the relevant point for my analysis of virtue in trying to explain the role of the external goods as instruments. The practice of virtue necessitates the external goods. Noble acts are not possible without external resources. The interpreter needs to take into account the instrumentality of the external goods in relation to virtue at all times when Aristotle inquiries about the practice of virtue.

Aristotle focuses his analysis of virtue towards an understanding of "how we are to act rightly" (*EN* II.2, 1103b30). Acting rightly is acting in conformity with right principle (*EN* II.2, 1103b32) and observing the mean (*EN* II.2, 1104a26). This makes sure that the external goods are not used badly but for preserving and enhancing our moral qualities and the good of others. Excess and deficiency destroy the moral qualities of people. The same actions can both generate and foster the virtues, they also can destroy them (if the mean is not observed), but also the virtues will find "their full exercise in the same actions" (*EN* II.2, 1104a28).

Acts themselves and the agent himself have to be of a certain sort: the acts have to be in conformity with virtues, and the agent in a certain state of mind, which is acting with knowledge, choosing to act for its own sake, and the disposition of character as the source of his actions (*EN* II.4, 1105a32–34). The repeated performance of just and temperate acts results in virtue (*EN* II.4, 1105b4). For Aristotle, virtue is "a mean state" (*EN* II.6, 1106b27), a "settled disposition of the mind" (*EN* II.6, 1106b35) between two vices; it avoids to "fall short of or exceed what is right" (*EN* II.6, 1106b17). A "just action" (*EN* V.5, 1133b30) is choosing what is equally removed from the two opposite. Someone's activity has to be marked by this standard found "between excess and defect" (*EN* VI.1, 1138b25).

These observations about how Aristotle understands virtue and its formation show the place of action in the whole process. The practice of virtue necessitates external goods, it leads to character formation and also makes sure that these external goods are used properly for edification not destruction. I can say that the external goods in the life of a virtuous man are tools both for noble acts themselves and for personal edification (this is how the actualizing virtuous activity, εὐδαιμονία, advances towards higher stages of actuality). Thus, the external goods as instruments are part of the process that makes personal virtue possible and public virtue possible. By public virtue I mean virtuous acts directed towards others. The external goods as instruments are an essential element in both of these directions:

internal towards character formation by habituation, and external towards the edification of others.

This interpretation of the instrumentality of the external goods is more comprehensive than the usual interpretation proposed by the inclusivist scholars who argue that the external goods are the consequence of a virtuous life,[22] or of the monist scholars who argue that the external goods are the condition needed for the exercise of happiness.[23] Also, my interpretation does not go that far as Bush's interpretation which says that happiness requires external goods to perform noble actions of virtue, and that these actions of virtue are happiness.[24] This understanding of happiness in terms of moral virtue was already dismissed by Aristotle when he discarded virtue as not being the ultimate self-sufficient end.

Thus, the usual alternatives of virtue and fortune, for explaining what happiness needs to thrive, can be nuanced with the ambivalence of the instrumentality of the external goods. They are needed both for the practice of virtue, and for the edification of character; they are tools for our own edification and for the edification of others. My interpretation also differs from that of some monists scholars who argue that the external goods are needed as instruments only by those people who devote themselves to perform virtuous actions on a grand scale.[25] This is true especially about the politicians.[26] As I will explain in the next section, I interpret the three mentioned externals of friends, wealth, and political power together as the necessary tools for accomplishing the public good, but these external goods can be present in the life of usual virtuous people, not necessarily only in the life of the elites.

To sum up, so far I have argued, in dialogue with the monist scholars, that the external goods as instruments are not simply the conditions for the practice of virtue, and in dialogue with the inclusivist scholars, that the external goods as instruments are not simply the consequence of the virtuous practice. The instrumentality of the external goods for the practice of virtue needs to be explained by taking into account the nature of action in the practice of virtue. The instrumental status of the external goods is not simply external to happiness, but part of the process through which virtues

22. Cooper, "Aristotle on the Goods of Fortune," 195.
23. Broadie, *Ethics with Aristotle*, 54; Höffe, *Aristotle*, 149.
24. Bush, "Divine and Human Happiness," 60.
25. Richardson Lear, *Happy Lives*, 180.
26. Richardson Lear, *Happy Lives*, 181.

are formed, and this process is actually a central aspect of εὐδαιμονία as the actualizing virtuous activity.

In our text from *EN* I.8, Aristotle mentions three external goods specifically: friends, riches and political power. Every one of these externals is different, and in the next subsections, I will analyze how every one of them is a tool for performing noble acts. I will argue that these specific three externals have, one the one hand, to be interpreted together as indicators of moral high status, and, on the other hand, they point to the necessary equipment for the practice of virtue.

5.3.1 Friends as Instruments of Virtue

Aristotle mentions friends as instruments to perform noble acts. Good acts can be performed by virtuous people who are willing to help others or contributing to the life of their family or larger group. In our text of *EN* I.8 it seems that for performing the mentioned noble acts, one person is not enough; a virtuous person needs the help of his/her friends. This is so because the task is beyond the abilities of one person,[27] it needs the cooperation of friends, and I add here, friends in high places. I add this because I interpret these three external goods (friends, riches, and political power) together. These friends have riches and are powerful politicians.

Thus, the mentioned noble acts (*EN* I.8, 1099a34) are acts for the good of the city. There is agreement between the inclusivist and monist scholars at this point. For example, the inclusivist scholars interpret the noble acts in our text as referring to "public and private philanthropy,"[28] and the monist scholars interpret the noble acts mainly as "political projects."[29] Historically, this is the case too: Aspasius (100–150 AD), says that friends are needed to overthrow tyranny; so, again the good of the city is in view.[30] The most likely reference of these external goods mentioned in our text from *EN* I.8 is to mature people of virtuous character, eligible for political responsibility.[31]

---

27. See also Sherman, who says that "we depend upon the aid and support of friends for accomplishing ends we cannot realize on our own" (Sherman, *Fabric of Character*, 126).
28. Cooper, "Aristotle on the Goods of Fortune," 179.
29. Kraut, *Aristotle on the Human Good*, 255.
30. Aspasius, *On Aristotle*, 25.
31. Roche, "Happiness and External Goods," 51.

If this is the case, we do not have here an egotistical use of others for personal gain, but the mature noble acts of helping others in the city or the city itself.[32] Because Aristotle here speaks about the practice of virtue, the use of friends as instruments is not an egotistical act. Implicitly here, Aristotle describes happiness as needing the virtuous performance of those who are in power, who are rich and who are friendly. Thus, these three external goods are not randomly chosen, but they are political indicators of high status.

Another element that needs to be discussed here is the nature of friendship as it relates to virtue, as understood by Aristotle. This needs to be addressed because Aristotle works with a direct connection between friends and the practice of virtue. This relationship between friendship and virtue is interpreted by the inclusivist scholars as follows: for someone to experience virtue s/he needs the context or the arena of friendship; as we are social beings, friendship structures the good life.[33] Friends as instrumental goods are those who benefit from the fine actions of someone else.[34]

In my analysis of how virtue, as the excellence of the soul, is achieved and practiced, I have focused on the practice of mean. This is relevant at this point as Aristotle says that, in social life, when a person practices the mean, that person will be a friendly person (*EN* IV.6, 1126b22). Such a person will behave like a friend and will be concerned with pleasures and concerns of social life (*EN* IV.6, 1126b31).

Thus, when a person practices virtues s/he will be good towards others.[35] For Aristotle, a friend is someone who "does what is good for the sake of his friend," and someone who "wishes his friend to exist and live for his sake" (*EN* IX.4, 1166a6–8, Ross). The relevancy of these points for my analysis of friends as external goods is that they are most likely virtuous too.[36] Friendship is built among similar people[37] because they are virtuous

---

32. See here the analysis of Shields who inquiries about the opportunity of having friends if we see them as "mere instruments to our own pleasure, toys to be played with when they suit our interests" (Shields, *Aristotle*, 394).

33. Sherman, *Fabric of Character*, 127.

34. Crisp, "Introduction," xxx.

35. See also Crisp, who says that "friendship involves goodwill" (Crisp, "Introduction," xxx), and Price, who says that "goodwill is a beginning of friendship" (Price, *Virtue and Reason*, 63).

36. See also Sherman who says that for Aristotle the primary focus is that of "virtue friendship" (Sherman, *Fabric of Character*, 125).

37. See also Broadie who says that "the best type of friendship is between virtuous

(*EN* VIII.1, 1155a4). A sensible decision made by every human being, both rich and poor, is to have friends (*EN* VIII.1, 1155a6) because in good times they will be "an outlet for beneficence," and in bad times they will be their only "resource," and for a young person a friend is "an aid," and for an old person a friend is "a supplement" (*EN* VIII.1, 1155a9–15).[38] As a means, Aristotle says, friendship is indispensable (*EN* VIII.1, 1155a29). Thus, for someone knowing Aristotle's complex understanding of virtue, his mentioning of friends, as an external good that needs to be added to happiness, is something expected; no one can live a virtuous life without friends. Thus, my conclusion is close to that of Sherman but following a different route, that of the centrality of the practice of mean.

5.3.2 Wealth as Instrument of Virtue

Riches or wealth are needed to practice virtue. As Aspasius said long time ago, in time of famine some have saved their country with their wealth or paid the ransom for the release of their parents.[39] A virtuous person can use his wealth for the good of others. Otherwise, if the person is not virtuous, s/he can use the riches for bad things, such as war, destruction or self-indulgence. I explain the relationship between the instrumentality of wealth and virtue by focusing on the practice of the mean. The mean will keep virtue in control of how wealth is used. This is what Aristotle says in Book IV: the mean in regard to wealth is the virtue of liberality (*EN* IV.1, 1119b22).

Because Aristotle speaks about wealth or riches, which means a great amount of value/money, I need to mention another virtue that might be in view here, magnificence. A similar connection is made by Höffe: the great wealth of a someone may increase the virtue of his generosity to make it magnanimity.[40] When a person engages in actions that involve expenditure on a large scale, Aristotle says, virtue is practiced when a "fitting expenditure" is done. By this he means that it fits the agent (a wealthy person), the circumstances and the object (a great cause) (*EN* IV.2, 1122a25–30). A wealthy person will spend a great amount of wealth to achieve things on a

---

individuals" (Broadie, *Ethics with Aristotle*, 23).

38. Sherman, *Fabric of Character*, 126.

39. Aspasius, *On Aristotle*, 25.

40. Höffe, *Aristotle*, 149.

great scale, and this will be how the virtue of magnificence is practiced. The public good is achieved in this way.[41]

The fact that magnificence might be in view here makes the monist interpreter confident that, for Aristotle, εὐδαιμονία is not an inclusive good. This is the argument: for the inclusive interpretation the happy person must possess every virtue. One of the virtues is magnificence, which requires great wealth. The implication is that only the wealthy person can be happy, which contradicts what Aristotle believes (*EN* X.8, 1178b33–1179b17).[42] Thus, the instrumentality of wealth to achieve virtue needs to be interpreted only in terms of equipment. As the instrumentality of wealth to perform noble acts is concerned all scholars agree that virtuous character is needed.[43]

5.3.3 Political Power as Instrument of Virtue

Noble acts are achieved sometimes with the help of powerful people. Aristotle understands the political leaders as instruments for virtuous action. The political power has the main purpose in helping the people of the city achieve the ultimate good in their lives.[44] Aristotle does not focus on a particular office of the political establishment but makes a general point underling the need for help from the top people in the city.

No great actions in one city are possible without some involvement of the political power of that place.[45] This need for political help shows the element of power that has to be active if the public good is going to happen. Otherwise virtue is practiced only in the private sphere of individual life.

---

41. See also Meyer who says that "liberality and magnificence concern the pursuit, expenditure, and display of wealth in service of family, friends, and the common good" (Meyer, "Living," 54).

42. Heinaman, "*Eudaimonia* and Self-Sufficiency," 50.

43. See for example Russell who says that "the use of wealth . . . count as goods for virtuous persons insofar as they are transformed into ongoing patterns of virtuous activity" (Russell, *Happiness for Humans*, 132).

44. Rowe, "Historical Introduction," 8.

45. Aspasius, *On Aristotle*, 25.

5.3.4 Conclusion

In this section about external goods as instruments of virtue I have argued for the following points: (1) The instrumentality of the external goods is a major factor for the possibility of εὐδαιμονία as actualizing virtuous activity; this is so because, according to Aristotle the things we do are the things we become. (2) The external goods are tools both for virtuous acts and for personal edification, they are instruments both for personal virtue and for public virtue. And (3) the external goods as instruments are indicators of high moral status and they point to the necessary equipment for the practice of virtue.[46]

---

46. See *EN* I.8, 1098b30, Rackham.

CHAPTER 6

A CONSTITUTIVE DEPENDENCY

6.1 INTRODUCTION

As I have said previously, in *EN* I.8, Aristotle gives two different reasons for the need of external goods, one positive and one negative. (1) The positive reason is given with the help of an analogy, that of instruments; as we use instruments to do various tasks, so we use friends, wealth, and political power to do many actions. (2) The negative reason is given to say what happens when we are deprived of certain externals: our blessedness is marred.[1] I have studied the first in chapter 5, and now I will study the second reason for the need of external goods. Let us read again what Aristotle says in *EN* I.8:

> Again, (1) being deprived of some things—such as high birth, noble children, beauty—spoils our blessedness (ῥυπαίνουσι τὸ μακάριον).[2] For (2) the person who is terribly ugly, of low

---

1. See also Broadie, who says: "There are two reasons why lack of external goods conflicts with happiness: (1) such goods are enabling conditions for excellent activities; and (2) some are such that their absence is a blight even the excellent activities can be carried on without them" (Broadie, "Book I," 281).

2. Other scholars translate this phrase as follows: "sullies supreme felicity" (Rackham); "takes the lustre from blessedness," (Ross and Urmson); "mars our blessedness" (Irwin); "disfigure their blessedness" (Bartlett and Collins); "disfigures blessedness"

> birth, or solitary and childless is not really the sort to be happy (εὐδαιμονικὸς),[3] (3) still less perhaps if he has children or friends who are thoroughly bad, or good but dead. As we have said, then, there seem to be an additional need for some sort of prosperity like this. (*EN* I.8, 1099b2–6, Crisp)

This is the text with the most problems to solve in the inquiry about the topic of external goods and happiness in *EN*. Mainly, it is an argument *via negativa*, which is an argument that explains how it is blessedness and happiness when some things are absent. But the details of the argument are more intricate. Here is why. The statement (1) is the main statement of the text, and it describes what happens to blessedness when good birth, good children, and beauty are absent: blessedness is marred/soiled. Then, by what it seems to be an explanatory reason for the statement (1), Aristotle presents the supporting statement (2) in which someone is not beautiful (utterly ugly), without a good birth (ill-born), without friends (solitary), and without children (childless). Such a person, Aristotle says, cannot be characterized as happy. Then, Aristotle presents the situation (3) as another supporting statement to (1) in which he goes further with his argument and speaks about someone who does not have good children or good friends (but utterly bad ones), and has lost good children or friends by death, such a person is less likely to be characterized as happy; in the statement (3) there are two scenarios: one in which someone does not have good children or friends, but utterly bad ones, and one in which someone had good children or friends, but they died.

Thus, Aristotle here describes contingent situations of fortune to explain why the external goods have to be added to happiness. There are things in life that are beyond the power of our actions, things that are not under our control, or under the control of virtue. For example, none of us can decide the family in which we are born, or if we are handsome or not. Even if we do our best to educate our children, in the end they choose what kind of persons they become. Also, no one can stop death in taking the good kids or friends away from us. So, the unpredictable role of fortune needs to be addressed in relation to our topic: external goods and happiness. Because of its unpredictability, fortune is hard to deal with. We do not

---

(Reeve); "like a stain on happiness" (Rowe).

3. Other scholars translate this phrase as follows: "hardly happy" (Ross and Urmson); "the character of happiness" (Irwin); "cannot really be characterized as happy" (Bartlett and Collins); "the stamp of happiness" (Reeve); "to call happy" (Rowe).

know if it is permanent or not, if it is decisive or not, or how quick the turn of fortune might be or ever be over. Nonetheless, fortune is part of life and needs to be discussed in relation to blessedness and happiness.

I identify the following issues that need our attention: (a) Why is it that Aristotle does *not* use εὐδαιμονία in this text, but μακάριον? Are these two terms synonymous in this text, or the interpreter needs to preserve them somewhat with different meanings? (b) What is the exact meaning of ῥυπαίνω (defile, disfigure) here, and what are the implications for blessedness? (c) What kind of understanding of fortune Aristotle exhibits here? And (d) when all of these issues are explained, how far would they be applied to explain the relationship between external goods and happiness? This is the road map for this section. I will approach every one of these issues and discuss them in dialog with the monist and inclusivist scholars, and by following the structure of Aristotle's text with these main three statements: (1) soiled blessedness, (2) being hardly happy, and (3) less likely to be happy.

6.2 MARRED BLESSEDNESS

This section is long and is organized with focus on (1) the meaning of blessedness and how blessedness is soiled by the absence (2) of good birth, (3) good children, and (4) beauty. In every one of these subsections I explore the larger Aristotelian context of ideas and then I engage with various scholars and their contributions. I will argue that blessedness refers to the pleasure aspect of happiness, and the absence of prestigious lineage, good education and discipline, and the appreciated goods of glory, honor and lack of pain, as important constituents of blessedness, soil it.

I start by mentioning the fact that, Aristotle does not use εὐδαιμονία in his saying ("spoils our blessedness"), and that this requires an explanation. The most common explanation is that Aristotle uses the terms blessedness (μαρκάριος) and happiness (εὐδαιμονία) interchangeably here. Before I analyze the debate, I need to point out what is at stake here. If these two terms are not synonymous here, does it mean that the absence or the loos of the external goods do not have an impact upon happiness? If the whole discussion is about blessedness and not about happiness, then the external goods are not constituents of it? This seems to be a strong argument for the monist interpreter. But if these two terms are used interchangeably here, then the absence or the loos of the external goods has a great impact upon happiness, and the chances of interpreting them as being part of happiness are great. Or, if these two terms share some common ground of meaning and have their specificity, then the implication is that whatever is specific to blessedness is affected by fortune. So, this is not a pure technical discussion, but one with important implications for the understanding of the relationship between the external goods and happiness in Aristotle's inquiry.

The argument for the interchangeable usage between εὐδαιμονία and τὸ μακάριον here in *EN* I.8 is as follows: Aristotle speaks about the same idea in the whole paragraph. Every one of his statements supports the first one: "being deprived of some things—such as high birth, noble children, beauty—spoils our blessedness" (*EN* I.8, 1099b2). There is no signal that he changes the subject, from happiness to something else.[4] Nonetheless, this argument is not decisive because it does not explain *why* Aristotle choose to use a different key term to describe what is impacted by fortune, namely blessedness. What is needed is a complete study of Aristotle's usage of τὸ μακάριον in *EN*, especially in connection to fortune and εὐδαιμονία, and based on this study the interpreter will see how these two terms compare with each other, if they are synonymous or not, if they share common ground of meaning or not. This is how the interpreter will assess *what* is soiled.

In *EN*, Aristotle has a varied usage of τὸ μακάριον.[5] I point out, (1) that Aristotle, in *EN*, can use these two terms, τὸ μακάριον and εὐδαιμονία, together in the same statement communicating two slightly different meanings. A good example is: "The gods, as we conceive them, enjoy supreme felicity and happiness" (*EN* X.8, 1178b9, Rackham).[6] No translator interprets the καὶ ("and") as epexegetical to translate as "gods are blessed

---

4. See also Roche, "Happiness and External Goods," 47, 58; Cooper, "Aristotle on the Goods of Fortune," 58; Russell, *Happiness for Humans*, 129; Paulo, "Aristotle's Understanding," 248; Majithia, "Aristotle on the Good Life," 64; Nussbaum, *Fragility of Goodness*, 329.

5. *EN* 1098a19; 1099b2, 18; 1100a33; 1100b16, 29; 1101a7, 19; 1101b5; 1113b15–16; 1152b7; 1157b21; 1158a22; 1169b4, 17, 24; 1170a2, 8, 27; 1176a27; 1178b9, 22, 26; 1179a2; cf. *TLG Workplace 7.0*.

6. Other scholars translate this text as follows: "Our belief is that the gods are blessed and happy to the highest degree" (Rowe); "We assume the gods to be above all other beings blessed and happy" (Ross and Urmson); "For we traditionally suppose that the gods more than anyone else are blessed and happy" (Irwin); "We assume the gods to be supremely blessed and happy" (Crisp); "we have supposed that the gods especially are blessed and happy" (Bartlett and Collins); "The gods, in fact, we supposed to be the most blessed and happy" (Reeve).

that is happy." Every major English translation leaves these two terms with distinct meaning. Nonetheless, it seems they are close in what they convey. For example, Bush says that these two terms are used here interchangeably but they are not synonyms. According to Bush, blessedness is seen by Aristotle "more immediately related to pleasure than happiness."[7] Bush does not give the necessary details to defend this nuance of meaning but, as I will show below, generally, he is right in his assessment.

Then, (2) Aristotle gives the reader an explanation about the meaning of τὸ μακάριον in *EN* VI.11, 1152b7. In this text Aristotle examines the nature of pleasure and pain; he says that "most people hold that pleasure is a necessary adjunct of Happiness, which is why the word denoting "supreme bliss" [τὸν μακάριον] is derived from the verb meaning "to enjoy" [τοῦ χαίρειν]."[8] It is surprising that the scholars do not give attention to this, apparently accepted, insight provided by Aristotle when the meaning of blessedness is assessed in *EN*. Based on such an insight, Bush's assessment with focus on pleasure is correct. Blessedness, understood in terms of pleasure and joy, is involved in happiness; blessedness is the pleasure dimension of happiness.

The question of interest for my inquiry is how Aristotle understands these two terms, blessedness and happiness, in the context of fortune and its impact in human life. The relevant text is found in *EN* I.10, 1100b1–1101a7. In this long text Aristotle assumes several things about εὐδαιμονία: it is permanent, it cannot be easily changed, it is determined by excellent activities (*EN* I.10, 1100b2, 9). When great good events take place in someone's life, that life is blessed [μακαριώτερον]. Those great good events add beauty to life (*EN* I.10, 1100b26). When a change of fortune happens and great bad events take place, they will "crush and maim blessedness" [θλίβει καὶ λυμαίνεται τὸ μακάριον]. Those great bad events will bring pain to life

---

7. Bush, "Divine and Human Happiness," 58.

8. Other scholars translate this text as follows: "most people say that happiness involves pleasure; this is why the blessed man is called by a name derived from a word meaning enjoyment" (Ross and Urmson); "most people think happiness involves pleasure—that is why they also call the blessed person by that name (*makarios*) from enjoyment (*chairein*)" (Irwin); "most people claim that happiness involves pleasure; that is why people call the blessed (*makarios*) person by that name, from *chairein* (to enjoy)" (Crisp; "most people assert that happiness is accompanied by pleasure. Hence, they have even derived the name of the "blessed" person from the feeling of "enjoyment"" (Bartlett and Collins); "most people say that happiness involves pleasure. That is why a *makarios* ("blessed") person is so called, after *chairein* ("to enjoy")" (Reeve).

(*EN* I.10, 1100b28). These great misfortunes are a time of pain, but even in them "nobility shines through" (*EN* I.10, 1100b29).

Thus, the pleasure/blessedness is maimed through pain, but nobility and greatness of soul are not. That is why, the blessed man cannot become miserable. A noble person with a great soul will not do bad acts. Such a good person will do the best in those circumstances of pain and hindrance. Pain is present, blessedness is maimed, but misery does not happen.

Thus, when I apply these insights to the meaning of the phrase, "There are certain external advantages, the lack of which sullies supreme felicity" [τὸ μακάριον] (*EN* I.8, 1099b2, Rackham), my explanation is as follows: good birth, good children, and personal beauty bring pleasure as happiness is concerned. When these external goods are absent, that good person does not experience pleasure and joy; in such a case, pleasure and joy are spoiled. Because of its importance and difficulty, this insight needs to be addressed in more detail by looking closer to the mentioned external goods and how they play their part in bringing pleasure.

6.2.1 Blessedness and the Lack of Good Birth

It is surprising that the major studies on external goods do not provide in depth studies into the Aristotle's understanding of good birth (εὐγένεια).[9] I will fill in the research at this point with the below inquiry. This subsection is organized around four things about the good birth in the Aristotelian corpus: definition, effects on character, relationship to politics, and relationship to happiness and fortune. I will argue that good birth as an external good is an intrinsic factor of life, and that is why, it has to be seen as potentiality for good character through actualizing activity which is happiness.

Aristotle defines εὐγένεια/good birth as meaning "coming from a fine stock" (*Rhetoric* 1390b22, Roberts). Such a concept is tense even in a time when slavery was widespread. The differences between rich/free, and poor/slave are deep, and they are talked about. They have implications in how citizenship is seen in the city. For example, Aristotle says that someone

---

9. In the Aristotelian corpus the topic of "good birth" is widely mentioned: *Ath* 28.2.3; *EE* 1233a30; 1249a10; *EN* 1099b3; 1122b31; 1124a21; 1131a28; 1179b8; *HA* 488b17–18; *MM* 2.8.5.9; *Pol* 1255a27, 33, 35, 40; 1282b32, 37, 39; 1283a2, 16, 34–35, 37; 1283b19; 1290b13, 28; 1293b37; 1294a21; 1295b6; 1296b18; 1301b3, 40; 1302a1; *Rhet* 1360b20, 27, 31, 34; 1367b30; 1387a15, 30; 1389a1; 1390b16, 18, 21, 23; *Divis* 12.i.22; 13.i.11, 15, 16, 17; 13.ii.10, 22. See *TLG Workplace 7.0*.

who is well-born is a citizen in truer sense than someone who is low-born. Being well-born means being sprung from better ancestors, and this will likely lead to be a better person. Such a person is appreciated more as a citizen than one who is poor and uneducated. Aristotle's references about "good birth" are accompanied by references to education; these two concepts go together. For example, a good father is likely to have a good son, and good education or training is likely to lead to good character (*Rhetoric* 1367b29, Roberts). This is how "a good birth is an excellence of race" (*Politics* 1283a35–39, Jowett).

Aristotle speaks about (human) race in terms of character, and expects that race develops and becomes good. For someone to have good parents or grandparents is a great asset, because this "fine stock" will give that person a better start in life, namely will give both the kind and the environment for becoming a better human being. The fact that someone had better ancestors than someone else is not a guarantee that s/he will be a better human being than others, but it constitutes a good start; Aristotle says that such men "are likely to be better men." This better start in life based on coming from a "fine stock" is acknowledged in society as being composed of birth and education, accompanied by wealth (*Politics* 1293b35). These things are not widespread, but rare. Aristotle rhetorically asks: "In what city shall we find a hundred persons of good birth and of excellence?" (*Politics* 1302a1, Jowett). The implied answer is *not in many*, because, in comparison with the number of rich people, who abound everywhere, the good birth and excellence is a rare combination.

Thus, a good birth is a good of fortune. No one can decide in which family is born. But when someone is born in a lineage of notable ancestors his character is affected. According to Aristotle, this distinction given by the family affects the character in that it makes the person more ambitious. That person has from the start this ancestral distinction, and would like to add to it, to develop it more (*Rhetoric* 1390b16–17). Achieving more than your ancestors is a powerful internal drive because it leads to enhanced reputation, greatness, and prestige (*EN* IV.2, 1122b31). Thus, a good man of a good birth ends up being worthy of honor. His character formed by the power of arguments is possessed by excellence (*EN* X.1, 1179b9).

When this rich stock of ideas is presupposed in *EN* I.8, 1099b3 it can be seen that Aristotle works with an intrinsic understanding of the part played by the good birth in relation to blessedness. If blessedness is an essential aspect of happiness with focus on pleasure (see my argument in chapter 5.4.1), the lack of good birth will affect blessedness. Both the reputation, greatness, prestige, and character are missing, and the pleasure of the excellent man will be affected. The potentiality for greatness given by being sprung from a fine stock is absent, thus blessedness is spoiled. Thus, the point made by Aristotle is not that a human being, by his or her choices, cannot achieve certain virtues, because the good birth as a condition for happiness is absent.

Let me explain it more. It is not that good birth constitutes the entry point into a wealthy family, and through that wealth and position someone can achieve great things, and, as such virtue is practiced. No. Aristotle's idea is that good birth has to be seen as a way of speaking about a person of noble character with achieved potentiality for goodness and nobility. Blessedness is marred not because the great acts cannot be accomplished through the good birth as a condition for happiness.[10] Blessedness is marred because good birth as achieved potentiality of goodness is absent, it did not happen. In this way a good birth is a constituent element of the actualizing virtuous activity, which is happiness.

This constitutive interpretation of the relationship between "good birth" and blessedness is different from that of other inclusivist scholars in the following ways. For example, Cooper and Cruzer say that the good birth, as an external good, contributes to happiness by the facts that someone actually has it and by the virtuous actions done,[11] or that these goods of fortune prevent distractions that would otherwise prevent happiness.[12] The interpreter needs to show the link between being born from a good stock and blessedness. For Cooper, and others, blessedness is synonymous with happiness and these terms are used interchangeably here. But, as I shown above, that is not exactly the case. There are distinctions between these two terms and that needs to be identified as exactly as possible.[13] Based on these

---

10. However, even Heinaman, one of the most important monist scholars, acknowledges that "among external goods that are necessary conditions for *eudaimonia*, Aristotle includes items that are not instruments, such as good birth and good children (1099b3), and in these cases the notion of "using" the external goods simply makes no sense" (Heinaman, "*Eudaimonia* and Self-Sufficiency," 49).

11. Cooper, "Aristotle on the Goods of Fortune," 184.

12. Curzer, *Aristotle & Virtues*, 423.

13. See also the criticism of Cooper by Brown who says that Cooper's position does not explain "neither why the men, and not the lack of non-instrumental external goods per se, are somehow responsible for soiling blessedness, nor why the point is expressed in terms of soiled blessedness" (Brown, "Wishing for Fortune," 68).

distinctions, I argue that the absence of good birth takes the lustre of blessedness/pleasure through the fact that the potentiality for goodness is absent. The ambition for greatness, prestige and character is not present, and this leads to pleasure and joy being soiled. This interpretation is different from that of Nussbaum who says that, when certain necessary conditions for good living are absent, their absence is an impediment to good living itself; fine actions cannot be done, and good living consists in them.[14]

Cooper, Curzer, and Nussbaum try to link the fact of good birth and good living with the help of good actions. My approach is different in that it is based on identifying the particularity of blessedness in relation to happiness, and on explaining the meaning of good birth as potentiality for goodness and greatness. And based on these two, I argue that the absence of good birth mars pleasure and joy because the achieved potentiality for goodness is not there. For example, there are slim chances for pleasure and joy in the life of a human being if that person does not have parents of good character and prestige offering him/her good education and nurturing. The good life of pleasure and joy is not possible if the good birth is not there. Aristotle does not say that pleasure and joy are impossible if the good birth is absent, but only that pleasure and joy are marred by the absence of good birth. Theoretically, it is possible to achieve a life of pleasure and joy, even if someone is not born from a good stock.

Also, I have to mention that, good birth is something no one can take away. Someone will always be the son or daughter of his/her prestigious parents. Wealth, beauty, children, friends can be lost, but good birth cannot; good birth is a permanent state. The only person that can destroy it is the person who has it. When that person chooses to live a life of vice, the ancestral notable excellent lineage will come to an end.

6.2.2 Blessedness and the Lack of Good Children

This subsection explores the link between the absence of good children and blessedness. I will explore how Aristotle understands the fact of having good children, how this depends on being a good parent, and how is their absence relevant to blessedness. I will argue that having good children is, in some measure, a reflection of the character of the parents; someone ends up with having good children if s/he is a good parent who took good care of them. Blessedness is soiled because the parent is not a person of good

---

14. Nussbaum, *Fragility of Goodness*, 339.

character and thus, his children are not good; this is how their pleasure and joy are disfigured by their bad character.

In his writings Aristotle does not develop too much the topic of "good children."[15] In *Rhetoric* 1360b-1361a, he speaks about it in the same context as here in *EN* I.8, 1099b. According to Aristotle, the "good children" are among the constituent parts of happiness. Good children mean children of good quality. The good quality refers to an excellent body (stature, beauty, strength, athletic power) and an excellent soul (temperance, courage) (*Rhetoric* 1361a1-4). The good children are not an exceptional concept found only in few, but it is expected to be found in large communities (*Rhetoric* 1361a10).

At the same time the fact of good children depends on good fortune. By good fortune Aristotle means the coming together of various circumstances in which someone can gain everything s/he can in the areas of family, happiness, and various physical advantages (*Rhetoric* 1391b1). This convergence of circumstances that leads to good times is beyond human control, that is why, Aristotle calls it good fortune.

These two aspects of our topic need to be explored together, by focusing on what a human can do. For Aristotle, what matters in relation to the larger topic of happiness is to take care of the property and of the body, making sure that they are in a good condition, and to make use of them (*Rhetoric* 1360b15). Someone ends up having good children because that person takes care of the body and the soul of his/her children. The body is harmoniously developed through work and physical exercise, and the soul is virtuously developed especially in the areas of temperance and courage. Bad events such as wars or famines, are beyond human control, and may happen, and they affect the good development of their physical and spiritual constitution. But Aristotle does not develop such exceptional circumstances and how they affect the character of children.

The relevant point for my inquiry is that the fact of having good children is in large measure the result of good nurturing and education. Having children of good stature and character is not beyond human reach. This accomplishment becomes a constituent of a parent's happiness.

Having good children is the wish of every parent, but it is a wish that can become reality, it is within reach, if the parent takes good care of his/

---

15. In the Aristotelian corpus the references to "good children" are as follows: *EN* 1099b3; *HA* 563b6; 614b33; 615a33; 616b24; 619b23; *Rhet* 1360b20, 39; 1361a1, 4; 1387a20; 1391a32. See *TLG Workplace 7.0*.

her children.[16] The good children bring joy to their parents, because they end up being respected and influential citizens in the public life of the city. When all of this is lacking, the joy and pleasure of a parent is soiled. At this point, Aristotle does not tell us how is it that good children are absent, if they were killed or if they were corrupted, or simply if the parents never had children (he will discuss the situation of having utterly bad children, or good children who died, in the second and third supporting statement of his argument). I suggest, for now, that the interpreter should understand the reference made to them in the same way as about the other two external goods mentioned here, good birth and beauty. Most likely, these were never a component of life of the persons Aristotle talks about in our first statement in *EN* I.8, 1099b3.[17]

In this way, I interpret them here in the first statement as things that never happened. I interpret them in this way because the good birth cannot be taken away by anyone, and if someone ended up having good children, the traits of character are well established and cannot be dislodged easily by misfortune (but in extreme situations through severe disaster, as Aristotle will mention in the third statement, good children might die). And it is the same about beauty, it is given. Not everyone has it. Aristotle does not develop the possible course of events in which someone's physical beauty is disfigured by an accident. When a human being is of good birth, has good children, and is beautiful, these goods are there to stay and cannot be dislodged easily.

This interpretation of mine is different from that of Brown in that these non-instrumental external goods are not simply the objects of wish that cannot happen. These non-instrumental external goods are *absent*. The point made by Aristotle is not that they are beyond our power to choose,[18] but that there are so many cases in which these goods are not part of

---

16. Brown makes reference to the same idea of wish, but interprets it differently, in that "even when children can be chosen, good children cannot" (Brown, "Wishing for Fortune," 70).

17. This interpretation is different from that of an inclusivist interpreter as Cooper who says that "the failure to have children would be a bad thing for him, and as such must be counted as detracting from the overall value of his life" (Cooper, "Aristotle on the Goods of Fortune," 180); and different from the interpretation of a monist interpreter as Kraut who says that "our blessedness is marred by defects in our social standing, family, and appearance because such disadvantages leave us less equipped than we would like to be as performers of fine actions. So, Aristotle is referring to the causal role of goods" (Kraut, *Aristotle on the Human Good*, 254).

18. Brown, "Wishing for Fortune," 70.

people's lives. That is the reason for which I interpret Aristotle's argument mainly as being a *via negativa* argument: what can be told about pleasure and then about happiness when some external goods are absent. The point is not about unfulfilled desires but about the implications of absence of non-instrumental constitutive external goods of pleasure and happiness.

I need now to explore the relationship between beauty and blessedness, as the third of the external good mentioned by Aristotle in his first statement of our text for understanding the meaning of its absence and how it mars pleasure.

6.2.3 Blessedness and the Lack of Beauty

This subsection explores the relationship between the absence of beauty and blessedness. Here I will fill in the present state of research by providing a more complete explanation of how Aristotle understand beauty, and how its absence soils blessedness. I will argue that beauty varies with age, but it is present at every stage of life; beauty is both a received blessing and an achieved blessing, and, in some measure is our responsibility achieving glory, honor and lack of pain at different stages in life, and thus being appreciated by others.

According to Aristotle, beauty,[19] as an external good, is a good of nature (*Rhetoric* 1362a4, 1387a15). Beauty is understood as referring to the symmetry of the body (*Topics* 116b21). This symmetry of limbs is pleasant to look at and constitutes an excellence of the body (*Rhetoric* 1362b14, 1388b14). Thus, the physical beauty is something desired of itself (*Topics* 118b21). Beauty does not need other qualities beyond itself to be desired. It is like health which in itself is desired. These two, beauty and health, make life pleasant. That is why, I will argue that, when beauty is absent, blessedness is marred.

But the human body changes through life, that is why, beauty varies with time of life (*Rhetoric* 1362b7). Thus, beauty will be a different thing, at different ages of the human body. For example, when a human being is young, beauty is to have a body that can run and contest well at the games;

---

19. The topic of beauty is explored by Aristotle in several of his writings: *EE* 1231a1; *EN* 1099b3; 1123b7; *MM* 1.2.1.4; 1.2.2.3; 2.3.15.1; *Mir* 837b22; *Mu* 391a20; *Ph* 246b7; *Protr* 4.4; 104.5; *Pol* 1254b39; 1282b37, 39; 1284b10; 1290b5; 1338b2; *Prob* 896b14; *Rhet* 1360b22; 1361a2, 6; 1361b7, 8; 1362a4; 1362b14; 1368a29; 1387a15, 28; 1388b14; 1405b6; 1407a1; 1413a34; *SE* 164b20; *SomnVig* 453b30; *Top* 116b18, 21; 118b21; *Divis* 2.i.2; 2.ii.3; 14.i.2, 11; 14.ii.2; 34.ii.12; 54.14; 61.11. See *TLG Workplace 7.0*.

thus, it is something pleasant to look at. When a human being is at his prime, beauty is being fit for war, and to have a formidable appearance as a warrior. When a human being is old, beauty is to be strong enough to move things at will, and to be free from pain. (*Rhetoric* 1361b7–16).

This comprehensive, age related, understanding of beauty, by Aristotle, is not found in the available scholarly research, but it is highly relevant for interpreting its absence, and its impact upon pleasure and joy (blessedness). According to this understanding of beauty as related to age, I argue that beauty is not an accident of nature,[20] but a constant quality of the body, as it goes through the stages of life. The beauty of the human body means different things at different ages. This is important, because we tend to understand beauty as mainly related to young and adult age, and not to the old age of life. Beauty can be absent at every age when someone is utterly ugly, as Aristotle will say in his second supporting statement of his argument here in *EN* I.8, 1099b. Thus, being well trained to compete in the games, being fit for war, and then having power to move things around make someone beautiful at different stages in life. When these features are absent, beauty is absent, and pleasure and joy are marred.

Thus, the absence of beauty at different ages is not something directly relevant to live a fulfilling sexual life (against),[21] but, mainly, is related to achieving glory at the games, honor in war, and absence of pain at old age. This is how the absence of beauty takes the lustre of blessedness. The fact of absence needs to be explored more in dialogue with the present scholarly research, both on the monist and inclusivist side of it.

6.2.4 Absence and Marring

In this subsection I gather the three previous subsections and interpret them together by focusing on the absence of good birth, good children, and beauty and how this soil blessedness. I will engage with the most important points made by various scholars, and I will argue for a constitutive interpretation of these goods; they mar pleasure and joy because they are intrinsic goods, constitutive of blessedness.

As I mentioned above, in the scholarly research at this point, the example put forward by Cooper (who defends an inclusivist/constitutive

---

20. Against Brown, who says that "physical beauty is also reasonably thought to be beyond our control" (Brown, "Wishing for Fortune," 70).
21. Cooper, "Aristotle on the Goods of Fortune," 182.

understanding of the external goods) is well known (and criticized): if a person is not of good birth or beauty s/he will not be able to secure sexual partners, and this will have an effect on how his or her temperance is developed.[22] This point is criticized by Brown (who defends an instrumental understanding of the external goods) who says that the overall approach of Cooper does not represent exactly what actually Aristotle does here. The point made by Aristotle, says Brown in criticizing Cooper, is that (1) the lack of non-instrumental goods *per se* is responsible for soiling blessedness and not what various men do, and (2) the blessedness being soiled is the phrase that needs to be explained not something else.[23]

The external goods that are absent (good birth, good children, beauty) are not objects of choice.[24] The reason for this is that every one of them is beyond our control. We do not decide in which family are born, we cannot guarantee how our children will turn out (good or bad), and our physical beauty is not a thing we decide. Thus, Brown says, these non-instrumental goods are only objects of wish. Our blessedness is soiled because of what society thinks about someone who is not of good birth, without good children, or not beautiful.[25] The "commonsense intuitions" of people around us will make our lives worse off when we lack these non-instrumental goods.[26] Happiness needs these non-instrumental goods because of social and psychological reasons[27]; so, the intuitions of others and the non-reachable wishes of our own are the reasons for which our blessedness is soiled when these non-instrumental goods are absent.

This criticism from Brown is with a strong impact. Unlike Cooper, Brown focuses on the fact that Aristotle speaks about the absence of these three externals goods and interprets them as objects of wish. It is true that they, commonly, are objects of wish, but Aristotle does not say *that* about them in our text. He says only one thing about them: they are *absent*. The fact of absence needs to be in focus when we interpret what Aristotle says here, not that they are absent, *and* we would like to have them.

---

22. Cooper, "Aristotle on the Goods of Fortune," 182.
23. Brown, "Wishing for Fortune," 68.
24. Brown, "Wishing for Fortune," 70.
25. This point of Brown is close to the point made by Kraut who says that when such external goods are missing, we are at disadvantage being less equipped; we are in a worse position to do fine things. See Kraut, *Aristotle on the Human Good*, 254.
26. Brown, "Wishing for Fortune," 74.
27. Brown, "Wishing for Fortune," 70.

My suggestion is that these absent external goods of good birth, good children, and beauty have to be explained by looking in the mirror. What I want to say is that, the interpreter needs to explore how it is when a human being has them, and then, by contrast, the interpreter will be able to show exactly what is absent from someone's life when they are not there. This is how their absence will explain the marring of blessedness/pleasure.

These external goods are goods of the body or goods of nature, and also, goods of fortune. There are features about them that make them blessings of nature, but at the same time, they are achieved blessings through education and discipline. Being born into a fine stock constitutes a good start, but this will be accompanied by the help of good, prestigious, and noble parents who provide good education and formation of good character for their children. The character of these good children is established well, and they are virtuous beings.

Thus, there are, so far, two perspectives mentioned through these two external goods. The first, is the good birth which anchors the person into a prestigious, good line of people. The external good of good birth constitutes an intrinsic good of nature which is understood as good potentiality for actualizing virtuous activity. Such a human being will continue to enhance the good character s/he has because of the good start of his/her good birth. Then, the second external good of good children will be a natural outcome too. As s/he had good parents who provided good discipline and education for him/her, in the same way s/he will do for his/her children. The fact that they end up being good children constitutes a relational good which brings pleasure and joy to their parents.

Then, the third external good, beauty is a good of the body. Because the human body goes through various changes in life, its beauty will go through various changes. A human being is beautiful at all ages (young, prime, and old age). The beautiful good-sized body is different at different stages in life. When a human being is young the beauty is being able to run well and win various contests, when the human being is in his prime, the beauty is to be fit for war, and when the human being is old, the beauty is to have strength to move at will and to be free from pain. This third external good brings the third perspective here; it is the aesthetic perspective. Beauty is an intrinsic good, which is both a received blessing, and an achieved blessing. The well-proportioned body is a received blessing, but it is a body that needs discipline, nurturing and formation. Then, especially at old age, it needs to preserve its strength and face well the ravages of old age.

Thus, the person Aristotle talks about in our text is most likely a mature person (he has good children) either in his prime or old age. It is a blessed person who is pleased with family, children and achievements throughout life. When these three external goods are absent this pleasure/blessedness is marred. This is how I explain the absence of these external goods, but I need to explain more exactly the meaning of "soiling/marring" of blessedness.

What does Aristotle mean by using this term translated in English as "marred/disfigured/soiled"? When the external goods of good birth, good children and beauty are lacking, this fact, Aristotle says, "takes the lustre from happiness" or "mars our blessedness" [ῥυπαίνουσι τὸ μακάριον] (*EN* I.8, 1099b2, Ross, Irwin). How should we understand this saying of Aristotle? 'Ρῠπαίνω means "defile, disfigure"[28] (our text from *EN* is specifically mentioned as having the meaning of "disfigure"). The lack of these externals (good birth, good children, beauty) "disfigure" our blessedness.

'Ρῠπαίνω is a rare term in the Aristotelian corpus: *Ath.* 6.4.1; *EN* 1099b2; *Rhet* 1405a24; *Fragmenta varia* 3.23.140.9.[29] I mention here the example of Solon found in the *Athenian Constitution*:

> for considering that [Solon, the master of affairs] was so moderate and public-spirited in the rest of his conduct that, when he had the opportunity to reduce one of the two parties to subjection and so to be tyrant of the city, he incurred the enmity of both, and valued honor and safety of the state more than his own aggrandizement, it is not probable that he besmirched [καταρρυπαίνειν] himself in such worthless trifles. (*Ath.* 6.4.1, Rackham)

The example of Solon shows us how it is when a virtuous man does not "besmirch" himself through acts of tyranny, but values honor and safety of the state more than his increase of power. For Solon, this would have meant a tainting transformation: a virtuous honorable man would have become a tyrant.

If I apply this insight to our text from *EN* I.8, the interpretation goes like this: in the situation in which good birth, good children and beauty are absent, blessedness/pleasure is changed/disfigured into sadness and pain. The pleasure and joy based on prestige, honor, character, both for himself and his children, and appreciated beauty at all ages, are transformed into pain. As I have argued above, rarely, if ever, a good birth can be lost, that

28. Liddell et al., *Greek-English Lexicon*, 1756.
29. *TLG Workplace 7.0.*

is why, in the second supporting affirmation of his argument, Aristotle will present the situation of low-birth. What I want to say is that, the absence of good birth is not to be understood as the decadence of a person of a good birth into a depraved person. The absence of good birth is the situation in which someone is of low birth. It is the same with good children. The absence of good children is the situation in which someone is childless or has utterly bad children. In an extreme situation, there is the situation in which a good child has died. When situations like these take place the blessedness is disfigured, that is the pleasure and joy turn into pain and sadness.

6.3 HARDLY HAPPY

This section is long and explains the second supporting statement of Aristotle. In it I will interpret the relationship between being utterly ugly, being ill-born, solitary, and childless, and happiness. When these facts are present, happiness is hardly possible. I will argue that the reason for this difficulty is the fact that these conditions are a description of utterly bad activities, lack of reason, envy, and lack of strong meaningful relationships. These are important impediments because the destroy virtuous character and activity, and, thus, happiness will be hardly possible.

The second statement of Aristotle's argument in *EN* I.8 says, "For the man who is very ugly in appearance or ill-born or solitary and childless is hardly happy" (*EN* I.8, 1099b4, Ross and Urmson). Aristotle puts together a portrait of a human being who does not have that much chance of being happy. This second statement is a supporting statement of the first statement in *EN* I.8: "There are some things the lack of which takes the lustre from blessedness, as good birth, satisfactory children, beauty" (*EN* I.8, 1099b1–3, Ross and Urmson).

This second statement speaks precisely about the happy man. There are these named situations that make happiness difficult to achieve. Aristotle does not say that it is impossible for such a person to be happy, but that happiness is hardly a possibility. The question that needs to be answered is why is this so? There are two main answers to it. (1) The monist interpreters argue that happiness is hardly a possibility for such a human being because the named conditions are impediments to virtuous action. Every one of these four situations make virtuous activity almost impossible. For example, if someone is utterly ugly, hardly anyone will be his friend or spend time with or work with him; thus, such a person ends up being solitary and without a context to practice virtue. Or if it is of low birth most likely will be poor and as such will not have resources to perform virtuous activities; also, it is possible in such a situation that his education and implicitly his character will be less developed and good. The other answer is (2) the inclusivist interpreters of happiness argue that these named conditions are not constituents of happiness and that is why such a person is hardly happy. Being utterly ugly, without education and character, alone, and childless make happiness almost impossible. I will evaluate these two answers in more depth after I offer the necessary research on these conditions in the whole Aristotelian corpus.

6.3.1 Happiness and Being Utterly Ugly

The term used by Aristotle that is translated as "utterly ugly" (παναισχής) is a very rare term. Actually, the usage in *EN* I.8, 1099b4 is a *hapax legomenon*, it is used only here, in the entire Aristotelian corpus. It is not used in the existing Ancient Greek Literature of the eighth, seventh, and sixth centuries BC.[30] In the fifth century BC it is used only once by Plato/Socrates in *Apology* 31b9:

> for I have neglected all my own affairs and have been enduring the neglect of my concerns all these years, but I am always busy in your interest, coming to each one of you individually like a father or an elder brother and urging you to care for virtue; now that is not like human conduct. If I derived any profit from this and received pay for these exhortations, there would be some sense in it; but now you yourselves see my accusers, though they accuse me of everything else in such a shameless way, have not been able to work themselves up to such a pitch of shamelessness (ἀπαναισχυντῆσαι) as to produce a witness to testify that I ever exacted or asked pay for anyone. For I think I have a sufficient witness that I speak the truth, namely, my poverty.[31]

Socrates's defense against his accusers makes the point that they did not degrade themselves by going that far and producing a witness to testify that Socrates took money for his teaching. That would have been "utterly ugly" or "a pitch of shamelessness." Historically, this is the first existing Ancient Greek text that we have to understand the meaning of this very rare

30. *TLG Workplace 7.0.*
31. Fowler, *Plato.*

term. This term (παναισχής) does not refer here to physical ugliness, but to ugliness of an action. Not even the accusers of Socrates were willing to go that far in their degradation. If this is the way to understand the term in *EN* I.8, then Aristotle's statement refers to an utterly ugly, shameless character of an action. This being the case, such a person cannot be happy, because, according to Aristotle, happiness is the virtuous activity of the soul. This meaning is confirmed by the other occurrence of παναισχής/utterly ugly in the fourth century BC: Demosthenes, *Or.* 54.33.9:

> Why should I? No; the man who was first to strike me and from whom I suffered the greatest indignity, he it is whom I am suing, whom I abhor, and whom I am now prosecuting. My words, then, are all true and are proved to be so, whereas the defendant, if he had not brought forward these witnesses, had, I take it, not an argument to advance, but would have had silently to undergo an immediate conviction. But it stands to reason, that these men, who have been partners in his drinking bouts and have shared in many deeds of this sort, have given false testimony. If mattes are to come to this pass, if once certain people shall prove shameless enough (ἀπαναισχυντήσωσίν) to give manifestly false testimony, and there shall be no advantage in the truth, it will be a terrible state of things.[32]

This text presents a legal battle against Conon by the plaintiff Ariston. Ariston was brutally beaten by Conon and stripped of his cloak. Ariston had the witness of Lysistratus, Paseas, Niceratus, and Diodorus to testify the truth about these facts. Conon had the apparently false witness of his drinking partners. This fact of testifying falsely is described by Demosthenes with the help of our term (παναισχής); such an action is utterly shameless. It can be seen that the term does not primarily refers to physical ugliness, but to the ugliness of an action. Based on these texts from Plato and Demosthenes, I argue that παναισχής/"utterly ugly" refers to an utterly ugly action, and the meaning in *EN* I.8, 1099b4, is "the man who is very ugly [in what he does]."[33] The fact that this term is used so rarely can be

---

32. DeWitt, *Demosthenes*.

33. It is surprising that the majority of translators (e.g., Irwin, Bartlett and Collins, Reeve) make reference to *physical appearance* as the main point made by Aristotle here. I say that this is surprising because the meaning given by the standard lexicon of Liddell, Scott, and Jones for αἶσχος is "ugliness, deformity, of mind and body" (Liddell et al., *Greek-English Lexicon*, 43). The exception is Crisp who translates "the person who is terribly ugly."

an indication of the fact that Aristotle refers to a rare condition in which the character of an action done by a person is utterly ugly, and in such a condition that person cannot be happy.

If Aristotle's point is mainly about the character of a human *action* and not primarily about human appearance, this fact guides the interpretation towards seeing human action, that is terribly ugly, making happiness hardly possible. In other words, such a person cannot be happy because his actions are not good, but utterly shameless. For someone to be happy s/he needs to perform virtuous actions not utterly shameless ones.

6.3.2 Happiness and Low Birth

Being born in a poor family, according to Aristotle, means low status in the life of the city. In such a situation of poverty and weakness it is difficult to guide your life according to reason (*Politics* 1295b8). From such a social condition of poverty, according to Aristotle, degradation happens. Such people end up envying those who have more than them or are better than them (*Politics* 1295b15–21). There is a clear distinction between freedom and nobility, and slavery and humble birth (*Politics* 1255b1). These are the associated ideas of "low birth" in the Aristotelian corpus.

Their relevance for my inquiry is that the lack of rational principle, and the presence of envy and roguery, makes happiness hardly possible. Happiness, according to Aristotle, is an activity guided by rational principle and virtue, and the fact of low birth usually does not lead to these factors in life.

6.3.3 Happiness and Living in Solitude

The fact of living in solitude and the possibility of happiness is analyzed by Aristotle by looking at the dispute whether the happy man needs friends or not (*EN* IX.8, 1169b1–20). This fact was debated at the time, because the self-sufficiency of the happy man can be misunderstood. It was assumed that the happy, self-sufficient man needs nothing from anyone because he already has the good things. Aristotle disputes this assertion based on two reasons: (1) a friend is "another self," and (2) the nature of man is to live with others.

Based on the fact that a friend is "another self," this "another self" provides things that cannot be provided by any human being through his/her own efforts. For example, when the times are good, friends are needed because they are thought to be the greatest of external goods. A good, happy man, when the fortune is kind, will bestow the benefits of his prosperity upon other people; such a person will practice generosity, and thus will enhance his virtue and his relationship with others. And when the times are bad and the fortune is not kind, such a man will need the help of his friends to get through this difficulty. Thus, friends are needed both in good and bad times. Having friends is both an opportunity to practice virtue in developing character, and in being the object of the virtuous activities of other people. That is why, solitude[34] is not a condition related to the character of a happy man.

The second reason given by Aristotle is the fact that man is a political creature and by nature lives with others (*EN* IX.8, 1169b18). Having friends is a natural necessity. Living in solitude goes against human nature. That is why, the solitary man cannot be happy. The good of man cannot be reached in solitude but only together with others. For a man to become good, he needs other people. Training in excellence is possible only in the company of other good people. This continuous context of virtuous reciprocal activities is necessary for happiness (*EN* IX.9, 1170a4–11).

Thus, self-sufficiency of the happy man does not exclude the presence of others, on the contrary, as I have argued in chapter 4, it has to be understood in relational social terms. The fact that a friend is another self, makes him/her necessary for a happy life, and the fact that a human being is a political creature, companionship is a natural necessity. That is why, a solitary human being can hardly be happy. Thus, solitude is an impediment for happiness because friendship is constitutive to happiness. What I want to say is this: when a human being does not have anyone else around him, this human being lacking an "another self" will not be able to live a happy life. The reason for this is that happiness includes friends. Friends are needed for a life of reciprocal, active actualized virtue.

---

34. Living a solitary life/μονώτης is mentioned by Aristotle in his writings in the following places: *EN* 1097b9; 1099b4; 1157b21; 1169b16; 1170a5; *HA* 625b9; cf. *TLG* Workplace 7.0.

6.3.4 Happiness and Being Childless

Being childless/ἄτεκνος,[35] as a moral concept, is not explored by Aristotle in his writings. There is one point made by Aristotle in *EN* VIII.12, 1162a28, that "childless people part more easily" that is relevant for my inquiry. The people with children has a strong relationship because their children are a common good. The thing that is common to them keeps them together. Thus, children are a "bond of union" (*EN* VIII.12, 1162a27).

Not having children means a weaker relationship between man and his wife. Aristotle explores the relationship between husband and wife as a friendship. This friendship exists by nature because, Aristotle says, a human being is naturally inclined to form couples (*EN* VIII.12, 1162a18). Thus, humans establish households with the aim of reproduction and with other various purposes; they help each other by bringing together their various gifts.

Their friendship brings them pleasure and utility. If both of them are good, the friendship between husband and wife also have the aspect of excellence. But being childless weakens this bond. The presence of children in a family constitutes a factor in a strong relationship. It is a non-instrumental good, constitutive in a strong relationship.

6.3.5 Happiness Hardly Achieved

Thus, I interpret this second supporting statement of Aristotle in *EN* I.8, 1099b, by focusing on (1) action, (2) status, and (3) relationships. For Aristotle, (1) happiness is the actualizing virtuous activity of the soul, and this activity will not be possible when people like Conon, and his drinking partners, are willing to commit the utterly shameful action of false witness. To practice such utterly bad action is to make the practice of happiness hardly possible. This interpretation of mine is different from all other interpretations[36] because it focuses not on *physical* appearance, but on the ut-

---

35. The references for ἄτεκνος in the Aristotelian corpus are as follows: *EN* 1099b4; 1162a28; *GA* 749a10; 755b19; 767a34; *HA* 577a3; 582b13; 636b8; *Pol* 1265a41; 1265b10; *Prob* 876b12; cf. *TLG Workplace 7.0*.

36. For example: Cooper, "Aristotle on the Goods of Fortune," 180; Kraut, *Aristotle on the Human Good*, 254; Sherman, *Fabric of Character*, 126; Richardson Lear, *Happy Lives*, 49; Irwin, "Permanent Happiness," 6; Halim, "Aristotle's Explanation," 110; Reeve, *Action, Contemplation, and Happiness*, 235; Roche, "Happiness and External Goods," 47; Brown, "Wishing for Fortune," 73–74.

terly ugliness of an *action*. Unfortunately, the scholarly research did not dig deep enough in this very rare term of Greek Ancient literature. I know that this is a very sharp criticism, but I make it with all due respect for my co-researchers and with one important thing in mind: the restless search for good understanding and truth; we follow Socrates's example and we search for truth together. Thus, my point here is that happiness is hardly possible because the subject of Aristotle's inquiry practices utterly ugly activities.

For Aristotle, (2) happiness will be hardly possible because the status of low birth makes someone to be irrational, rogue and envious. Being born in poverty, in a family of low status, it is very likely that good character and reason will not be developed. In such a condition of character, the virtuous rational actualizing activity of the soul will not be practiced. Thus, the impact of the low status is decisively intrinsic in being an impediment for happiness, and this low life does not belong to virtuous happy life.

For Aristotle, (3) happiness is a self-sufficient ultimate good, and I interpret this in relational social terms (see the argument in chapter 4). Because of this, happiness is possible in the context of strong relationships. When a human being lives in solitude, that person, because s/he lacks relationships, very likely will end up unhappy. Also, I interpret the fact of someone being childless in this larger context of relationships in life. When a man and his wife do not have children, Aristotle says, their bond is not strong. Being childless leads to weak relationships, because the children are the bond of a strong union between man and his wife, and this makes happiness hardly a possibility.

But Aristotle does not stop to these impediments that make happiness hardly a possibility, he goes further and add other stronger impediments that make happiness less likely possible. I will analyze them in the next subsection.

6.4 LESS LIKELY TO BE HAPPY

The third supporting statement of Aristotle goes further away as the possibility of happiness is concerned. Aristotle describes two situations that makes happiness very unlikely. When someone has utterly bad children or friends, and when someone had good children and friends, but they have died. These are the most unlikely situations in which someone can be happy. These situations are about others that are very close to him, and about their impact in his life. Why is this impact so powerful?

The monist interpreter says that, the utterly bad character of someone's children/friends, or the death of his good children/friends will bring pain, frustration, and will be an impediment for virtuous action, and these will make happiness very unlikely. The inclusivist interpreter says that, these situations are with such powerful impact because someone's children and friends are constituents of someone's happiness, and when they are utterly bad or good but dead, happiness is a very unlikely possibility. I will analyze every one of these two situations, and then, I will argue that (1) utterly bad character of children and friends is a reflection of the character of parents and friends, and (2) death takes away profound virtuous relationships that are constitutive of happiness, and these two facts (utterly bad character and death) make happiness very unlikely.

6.4.1 Happiness and Having Utterly Bad Children and Friends

This is the only place in his writings where Aristotle uses this term (utterly bad/πάγκακος).[37] For having a good understanding of the meaning of πάγκακος it helps to see how Plato uses it in *Laws* 743b4–7. Plato explains the fundamental purpose of laws in society as being the happiness of its citizens and their unity in friendship. He explores the relationship between being good and rich, and concludes that, a very rich person is not a good one. The reason for this, according to Plato, is that a good person will gain his wealth only by just means and will spend it on noble objects. Such a person will never end up very rich (neither very poor). According to Plato, the very rich person ended up like that because his wealth derives both from right and wrong means, and he will not spend it nobly; thus, he will end up with much more. In this context, Plato uses the term πάγκακος/ utterly bad, to describe the rich person who is not generous, and the poor person who is lavish. Plato's overall argument is that every man in the State needs to be concerned, first, with his soul, second, with his body, and third, with money.

---

37. In the existing Greek literature beginning with the eighth to the fifth century BC, πάγκακος occurs in the following texts: Hesiodus, *Epic. Op* 813 (eighth century); Theognis, *Eleg* 1.149; Aeschylus, *Trag. Th* 552; *Ch* 740 (sixth century); Euripides, *Trag. Fragmenta* 57.1; 666.1; 939.1; *Alexandri* 38.1; Sophocles, *Trag. Tr* 1124; *Ant* 742; Plato, *Polit* 300e1; *Prot* 334b4; *Leg* 743b4, 7; 928e3; *Ep* 354e4; Hippocrates, Med. et Corp, *Prorrheticon* 2.1.7 (fifth century). See *TLG Workplace* 7.0; Liddell et al., *Greek-English Lexicon*, 1284.

When I apply this understanding to what Aristotle says in *EN* I.8, 1099b, I say that, happiness is not a very likely prospect for a parent whose children are "utterly bad." These children are utterly bad in relation to their character. They do not practice the mean in their actions, and accordingly they are not virtuous human beings. Their condition makes their parents unhappy. But there is more than that.

The character of someone's children reflects, in some measure, the education that child received at home from his/her parents. There is some correspondence between the character of the parents and of their children. While no one can guarantee that his children will end up good, their chance of ending up good depends, in some measure, upon the education they have received from their parents. If the parents were utterly bad, their children will very likely end up like their parents.

It is the same with having utterly bad friends. Usually people are friends with people of similar character and interests. When someone has utterly bad friends that says something about his character. Aristotle does not say that someone has "bad" friends (or children), but someone has "utterly bad" friends or children. The term πάγκακος is translated "wholly evil" in the other two occurrences in Plato (*Laws* 928e3; *Letters* 354e4).[38] The point is that the character is entirely destroyed, moderation is abandoned, and immoderation is practiced. Such a parent or friend did not offer what they should to their children or friends. If they would have done it, Aristotle says, their relationship/friendship would have been abiding and excellent (*EN* VIII.7, 1158b23).

Thus, it is very likely that happiness is a very distant possibility because having utterly bad children and friends it is a reflection of the character of their parents or friends. Happiness is not possible when the character is destroyed, and someone is wholly evil. This is the reason for which this third supporting statement needs to be interpreted in constitutive terms: when the character is utterly bad, happiness is not possible.

6.4.2 Happiness and Having Good Children or Friends who Died

The other situation that Aristotle describes is the situation in which good children and friends die. The death of good children or friends makes the happiness of parents or friends very less likely. Why is this so? Aristotle offers his understanding of the relationship between death and virtue in

---

38. Bury, *Plato in Twelve Volumes.*

EN III.9, 1117b7–17. There he explains why a courageous person will be willing to die: because it is noble to do so, and base not to do so. According to Aristotle, even the moment of death is a reflection of his character.

But because of its finality, death is the most terrible of all things. Life is the greatest good, and its loss brings great pain. That is why, when a good child or friend die, the parents or his friend are not very likely to be happy. Two things are lost in such a circumstance: a profound virtuous relationship, and life, the greatest good. This loss makes happiness a very distant possibility. The good child/friend that is dead will no longer enjoy happiness, and the parent or friend will no longer have profound virtuous companionship which makes happiness possible. That is why, this kind of loss needs to be explained in constitutive terms, because the presence of good children and friends makes happiness possible.

6.4.3 Very Distant Happiness

Thus, these two very difficult scenarios of having utterly bad children/friends, and having good children/friends who have died, pose, Aristotle says, the greatest problem for happiness. When these things occur, happiness is very unlikely to be practiced. There is common ground between monist and inclusivist scholars when they explain the reason for which these circumstances have such a powerful impact against happiness. The monists scholars argue that when someone has bad children and friends, that person ends up in disgrace. The social attitudes of opprobrium towards him will affect his opportunities for virtuous action.[39] The inclusivist scholars will agree with these hard-social impediments for virtuous action,[40] and will add the factors of pain, frustration, and disappointment of the unsuccessful parents that make happiness a very distant possibility.[41]

But the inclusivist scholars will go further with their interpretation and will say that, when such external goods are bad or absent because of death, their condition or absence make happiness almost impossible because, they being valued for their own sake, they belong to a complete life[42]; or their absence impairs good living itself by impending virtuous activity

---

39. Kraut, *Aristotle on the Human Good*, 256.
40. Nussbaum, *Fragility of Goodness*, 328.
41. Cooper, "Aristotle on the Goods of Fortune," 180; Irwin, "Permanent Happiness," 6.
42. Irwin, "Permanent Happiness," 6.

in which good living consists. When such external goods are lost it makes life seen not worth living.[43]

My interpretation goes beyond the inclusivist interpretation by focusing on the following elements. (1) The fact that someone has utterly bad children or friends, that is, in some measure, a reflection of his/her own character. Thus, the focus is not so much on the frustration and disappointment of a parent or friend, but, in some measure, the focus is on their character. The children ended up utterly bad, because their parents have been bad; and someone's friends are utterly bad because s/he is being utterly bad has associated with them and continue to do so. So, this aspect of reciprocity of character formation is what I bring to the interpretation of this point made by Aristotle as the explanation for the almost impossibility of happiness in such circumstances. (2) When someone's good children or friends die, happiness is very less likely, not so much because they are being now dead constitutes an impediment for doing fine actions; and not being able to do fine actions makes happiness impossible because good living consists in practicing these actions. The reason is deeper than that. The relationship between good parents/friends and their children/friends is a reciprocal profound virtuous relationship. This reciprocal virtuous relationship makes happiness possible. When death happens, this reciprocal virtuous relationship is destroyed, and happiness is a very distant possibility. The focus is not so much on the pain (though no doubt that the pain is profound) but on the loss of a constitutive part of happiness as actualizing virtuous activity.

6.5 THE POLITICAL HUMANITY AND THE POLITICAL GOOD

This is my suggested solution to the question of why the loss of the external goods make the human good, happiness impossible. The instrumentalist monist answer to this question is that there is an indirect connection between happiness and these goods, and on instrumental grounds, when these goods are absent or lost, the agent no longer can practice the correspondent virtues. For example, when the good children die, happiness is no longer possible because the agent no longer can practice the virtue of fatherhood. The same with the death of friends; when they die, the agent can no longer practice the virtue of friendship, and thus, happiness is not possible. This instrumental monist interpretation of the absence of the external goods

---

43. Nussbaum, *Fragility of Goodness*, 331, 361.

is challenged by the constitutive inclusivist interpretation by arguing that these absent goods are intrinsic goods constitutive to happiness as activity. For example, when friends die, happiness is no longer possible because friendship as an activity is no longer possible, and thus, happiness is not possible. The decisive criticism from the instrumental interpretation upon the constitutive interpretation is that these absent goods are not activities done by the agent. Aristotle, the instrumental interpretation says, does not say that the agent does those things, only that they are absent or lost. This criticism is decisive, and the constitutive interpreters need to answer it.

I will suggest an answer to this challenge for defending a constitutive interpretation of the absence or the loss of the external goods, and the impossibility of happiness. My suggested solution is that the absence or the loss of these external goods make happiness impossible because these goods are constituents of our political humanity. When our political humanity is dismantled, our political good is no longer possible. For example, when the good children or the good friends die, happiness is impossible because the good children and the good friends, as components of our political humanity, are gone, and as such the political good, happiness, is no longer possible. The important link here is between our political humanity and our political good. This is how Aristotle sees us, and how he sees our good, both in political terms. The common aspect of this political perspective is the intrinsic relational aspect. We are what we are among and with others in the city, and our human good is the political good. The instrumental monistic interpretation is right in saying that Aristotle does not mention here any activity the agent does. Thus, the constitutive inclusivist interpretation, by arguing that these external goods are constituents of happiness as activity, loses ground in the debate. But if these goods are part of the human nature, the constitutive interpretation has an answer to the instrumentalist monist challenge.

Happiness as the political good is the good of the reigning science of Politics, it is ultimately the good of the city. The goods of all the sciences lead to the good of the science of Politics. From the perspective of an individual person, the link to this ultimate good of the city, the political good, is, according to our text in *EN* I.8, focused on our good lineage, good children, beauty, and good friends. In the city, these external goods, are important constituents. Every good city is composed of prestigious honorable families, which have well educated children, who are beautiful in that, when they are young, they win the games for their city, when they are adults, they win wars for their city, and when they are old, they can manage their lives by themselves and are not a burden for the city. These prestigious honorable families have as their good friends other prestigious honorable families, and in this way the city is a strong political network based on strong friendship. This is the link between these named external goods in *EN* I.8 and the good of the city, the political good.

When these external goods are absent, our political humanity is dismantled, and our political good, happiness, is no longer possible. The city is weak and fragmented, because there are no prestigious honorable families with well-educated children in it, no victories at the games and in wars, and no friendships but strife. The absent components of our political humanity make our political good an impossibility.

My suggested interpretation answers the challenge of the instrumentalist monist interpretation in the following way. I acknowledge that the named absent goods of good birth, good children, beauty, and good friends are not activities of the moral agent. That is why these cannot be intrinsic components of the activity of happiness. But they are intrinsic components of our political nature, from birth to death. That is why, when they are absent or lost, they dismantle our political humanity and make our political good impossible. These absent or lost external goods do not make happiness impossible because they, as objects of wish, are not attainable. These external goods are both received and acquired goods. Being born in a prestigious family does not guarantee good character, but it makes it very probable because, when education is provided and the willingness to learn and mature are present, a good character is formed, and they become good children. Such a person will develop good friendships and based on his good character will be a good citizen. As such the political good becomes possible. But when these external goods as components of our political humanity are absent or lost, happiness as the political good becomes impossible. Thus, I argue, the main point of Aristotle here is not that these external goods of good birth, good children, beauty, and good friends, by being absent make the practice of the correspondent virtues impossible, and indirectly, happiness impossible. I argue for a direct link between the absence of these constituents of our political humanity and the impossibility of our political good.

6.6 CONCLUSION

This chapter is my analysis, interpretation, and engagement with scholarship of the difficult text from *EN* I.8, 1099b, where Aristotle speaks about the role of the external goods in explaining his understanding of happiness. I interpret the dependency of happiness on external goods based on his two main reasons for the need to have the external goods added to happiness in the following way.

(1) I interpret it as an enhancing instrumental dependency in which the external goods are tools in a complex personal-public way. Happiness as the activity of the soul according to virtue depends on external goods in that these goods make happiness possible. What we practice has an impact upon our formation. We use the external goods as tools for our virtuous actions, and for our edification; they are instruments for our personal virtue and for public virtue. The external goods, as instruments, are indicators of high moral status, and they point to the necessary equipment for the practice of virtue. This is how happiness has an enhancing-instrumental dependency on external goods.

(2) I interpret it as a constitutive dependency in which the external goods, mainly, are constituents of our political nature, and as such, of the political good in a complex way. The pleasure aspect of happiness, blessedness, is marred by the absence of a prestigious, good line of people which constitutes an intrinsic political good of nature, a good potentiality for actualizing virtuous activity. Blessedness is marred by the absence of the natural outcome of a good birth (of the parent) towards his children which is good discipline and education, and so, they will become good. Blessedness is marred by the absence of beauty, which is an intrinsic good, which at different stages in life constitutes different things which bring various political benefits: glory, honor and absence of pain. Thus, I argue that here Aristotle speaks about a mature blessed person who is pleased with prestigious lineage, good children, and magnificent achievements throughout his life in the city. When these goods are absent from his political nature, the pleasure aspect of happiness is marred.

Aristotle will support this insight through two supporting statements. I interpret the first supporting statement by focusing on action, status, and relationships. Happiness is hardly possible because the subject of Aristotle's inquiry practices utterly ugly activities and as such is an utterly ugly person; the status of low birth makes him irrational, rogue, and envious; and the envisioned person here lacks the context of strong relationships in the city.

I interpret the second supporting statement by focusing on the fact of having utterly bad children or friends is, in some measure, a reflection of that person's character; the children end up being utterly bad, because, in some measure, their parents have been bad, or someone has utterly bad friends, because, in some measure, s/he is, in some measure, similar to them. I argue that, Aristotle here focuses on the reciprocity of character formation between parents and their children, and between friends. The other situation mentioned here is the death of good children or friends as a major impediment for happiness. My interpretation is that, the fact of their death is such a major impediment because death severs a very profound virtuous relationship between parents and their good children, and between virtuous friends. Happiness is possible because of this virtuous reciprocal relational political context, which is destroyed by death.

These insights about parents and children, loss and death are exemplified by Aristotle with the help of a legendary figure: Priam, the last king of Troy. Studying the example of King Priam and the disaster that happened to him is the topic of the next chapter.

CHAPTER 7

PRIAM'S LOSSES AND HAPPINESS

7.1 INTRODUCTION

PRIAM, AND WHAT HAPPENED to him, occurs at two key points in Aristotle's inquiry in *EN*. The first occurrence helps Aristotle's point that, happiness requires a complete lifetime, and Priam, apparently, does not qualify because, in his old age, he suffered great misfortunes.[1] The second occurrence confirms a point made by Aristotle that, on the one hand, severe misfortunes mar blessedness through pain and blockage of virtuous activities, but on the other hand, even in great misfortunes the nobility of a good and wise man will shine through. What happened to Priam shows exactly this very complex situation that needs nuances when it is explained. Here are the extended quotes that mention him:

> Happiness as we said, requires both complete goodness and a complete lifetime. For many reverses and vicissitudes of all sorts

1. See also Irwin, who says that "Aristotle suggests some connection between happiness and length of time; and we might think he regards a "complete time" as a lifetime. On this view, Priam's misfortunes in old age imply that he never was happy" (Irwin, "Permanent Happiness," 12). Also, Höffe, who says that "happiness remains at the mercy of a superior power.... This power [is perceived] as the embodiment of contingent accidents" (Höffe, *Aristotle*, 152). Baracchi makes the same point that happiness involves the assumption of a complete life. See Baracchi, *Aristotle's Ethics as First Philosophy*, 99.

> occur in the course of life, and it is possible that the most prosperous man may encounter great disasters in his declining years, as the story is told of Priam in the epics; but no one calls a man happy who meets with misfortunes like Priam's, and comes to a miserable end. (*EN* I.9, 1100a4–9, Rackham)

> And if, as we said, a man's life is determined by his activities, no supremely happy man can ever become miserable. For he will never do hateful or base actions, since we hold that the truly good and wise man will bear all kinds of fortune in a seemly way, and will always act in the noblest manner that the circumstances allow. . . . And this being so, the happy man can never become miserable; though it is true he will not be supremely blessed if he encounters the misfortunes of a Priam. Nor yet assuredly will he be variable and liable to change; for he will not be dislodged from his happiness easily, nor by ordinary misfortunes, but only by severe and frequent disasters, nor will he recover from such disasters and become happy again quickly, but only, if at all, after a long term of years, in which he has had time to compass high distinctions and achievements. (*EN* I.10, 1100b33–1101a14, Rackham)

Thus, how should we understand these references to Priam? Is it a test case?[2] Or a problem that has to be solved?[3] A paradigm for the virtuous man?[4] I presented these solutions to this complex issue in chapter 3. For my project, I need to inquire Priam, and what happened to him, because it offers insights about how Aristotle understands the dependency of happiness upon external goods. Priam, and what happened to him, is an example of what happens when a good, wise, and happy man loses everything (family, friends, wealth, power, and city).

The monist interpreters say that, Priam, by losing everything, is no longer able to perform virtuous actions. For example, the fact that his good son Hector is dead, is now an impediment for him to exercise the virtue of being a father.[5] The loss of a good son is interpreted in a different way by the inclusivist scholars, who say that the death of a good son is more than an impediment to virtuous action, this loss has an impact upon happiness

---

2. Nussbaum, *Fragility of Goodness*.
3. Russell, *Happiness for Humans*.
4. Halim, "Aristotle's Explanation."
5. Kraut, *Aristotle on the Human Good*, 256.

because the good son is valued for his own sake and is part of the best human life.⁶

My thesis is that, the external goods that are lost by Priam are both instrumental and constitutive to his happy life, and because of their loss, Priam is no longer supremely blessed. Every scholar agrees that they are instrumental in relation to happiness because with their help a happy person can perform virtuous actions. So, I will not discuss this aspect here. But I will argue that their constitutive role needs to be understood based on Aristotle's particular understanding of the self-sufficiency of happiness. I will argue that, because for Aristotle the self-sufficiency of happiness is a relational transformative concept, when a happy person loses his family, friends, and city his happiness is deeply impacted because one of its core qualities, self-sufficiency, is destroyed.

Aristotle understands the self-sufficiency of happiness as transforming relationships with others. For Priam, the good character is still there, the good actions are still possible (even if they are impeded by the loss of wealth and power), the wisdom is still there, but what is lost, at least for now, are the relationships with his family, friends and the city, who are gone or destroyed. These can be rebuilt, but it needs a long time. Thus, I will argue that the loss of the external goods of family, friends, and the city destroys the self-sufficiency of happiness. This destruction is not definitive, but it can be rebuilt through "high distinctions and achievements" (*EN* I.10, 1101a13).

I organize the argument for this thesis, in this chapter, by focusing on (1) Priam's losses, (2) their impact on his happiness, and (3) the relevance of Priam's misfortunes for understanding the role of the external goods in the life of a happy man.

7.2 PRIAM'S LOSSES

Aristotle's references in *EN* to Priam's loses⁷ are comprehensive. He assumes that the reader knows the details of the story in the epics (*EN* I.9, 1100a8). Aristotle makes references to Priam's misfortunes only in *EN*, that

---

6. Nussbaum, *Fragility of Goodness*, 256.

7. Priam is mentioned 17 times by Aristotle in his writings: *Ath* 47.2.12; *EN* 1100a8; 1101a8; 1145a21; *HA* 618b26; *Oec* 1346b12; *Rhet* 1362b36; 1363a6; 1414b39; 1416b2–3; *Fragmenta varia* 3.24.147.6; 5.30.191.75; 8.44.487.25; 8.45.611.359; 8.50.641.49, 63. See *TLG Workplace 7.0*.

is why, there is no help from other writings in understanding how the example of Priam functions in Aristotle's ethical inquiry.[8]

The comprehensive character of Priam's misfortunes is depicted by Aristotle by using phrases like: accidents of fortune, great and frequent reverses [of fortune], adversity, severe and frequent disasters (*EN* I.10, 1100b21–1101a14). The relevancy of this comprehensiveness is that everything that Priam had is now lost in various ways: accidents, reverses of fortunes, adversity, disasters. These are echoes of the complex story of Priam in the Trojan war, where Priam endures, in a passive way,[9] what happens to him with the focus of showing nobility and excellency of character. This is how Aristotle presents Priam, as someone whose nobility shines in adversity.[10] Losing everything does not destroy nobility. His family, his friends, his soldiers, and his city are lost, but his nobility is not. The virtue of his nobility cannot be practiced because the instruments of wealth and power are destroyed, but it can be seen in how he endures with patience the severity of loss.[11]

Thus, not even the loss of everything has the power to destroy character. It seems that Priam, for Aristotle in *EN*, functions as an example intended to prove how stable the virtues and character of the happy man are. I argue that, it seems that Aristotle works with a fine distinction between

---

8. It is somewhat similar with his master, Plato, who does not develop the case of Priam in any relevant way for ethics. The only text of Plato that makes reference to Priam's misfortunes is in *Rep* 388b4, where he quotes Homer's *Iliad* 18.23–24; 22.414–15; 24.3–12: "Not to represent Priam, a close descendant of the gods, as entreating his men and
Rolling around in dung,
Calling upon each man by name" (*Republic* 388b4, Grube).

9. See also Halim, who says that Priam is presented "as facing a basically passive misfortune, in the sense that his misfortune is something that he suffers rather than something that he does or that he brings upon himself" (Halim, "Aristotle's Explanation," 207).

10. See also Cooper, who says that "even in these circumstances fine character shines through, when someone bears many great misfortunes with a good temper, not because he does not feel distress but because he is noble and great in soul" (Cooper, "Aristotle on the Goods of Fortune," 188).

11. I mention here how Nussbaum envisaged the ways in which uncontrolled fortune interferes with virtuous activity: (1) it deprives it of some instrumental means, and (2) it may block activity by depriving it, not merely of an external instrument, but of the very object or recipient of activity. See Nussbaum, *Fragility of Goodness*, 327. Curzer approaches the relationship differently, saying that "luck is neither central nor irrelevant to happiness. Aristotle claims that luck plays a complex, important role, although virtuous activity is more central to happiness" (Curzer, *Aristotle & Virtues*, 419).

character and the expression of happiness. I have argued (see chapter 4) that Aristotle understands happiness as the actualizing activity of the virtuous soul, and now, because of the total loss, this virtuous activity cannot be exercised. But the impact is more severe, at a deeper level, and this is what I explore in the next section.

7.3 THE IMPACT UPON PRIAM'S HAPPINESS

Priam has lost everything: his family, friends, wealth, political power, and Troy. This comprehensive loss constitutes both pain and impediment. The suffering of the loss is overwhelming, and this is how his pleasure and joy/blessedness are marred. By losing his family, friends, wealth and political power he has lost the instruments for practicing virtue. But these external goods affect Priam's happiness in yet another way.

I will start exploring this aspect by making reference to Nussbaum's interpretation[12] of how this impact upon happiness needs to be seen. After Priam has lost everything, Nussbaum says, his capacity to act virtuously has been severely diminished; he no longer can exercise various excellencies for which he was previously known. But, by losing this sphere of activity, he has lost something deeper than mere contended feeling. The good character of Priam is still there because he continued to show it through his actions.[13] Priam was able to find a way of good behavior even in the worst circumstance, but in this extreme situation, not even this will prevent the loss of happiness.[14]

I compare this inclusive interpretation with that of Cashen[15] (a monist interpreter), who (1) interprets Priam's case as mainly belonging to the established interpretations (*endoxa*) at the time,[16] and (2) explains the impact of the loss of external goods in terms of (a) an impediment for virtuous

---

12. For a detailed presentation of Nussbaum's inclusive interpretation of how the external goods need to be seen in relation to happiness in EN, see chapter 3.

13. Nussbaum, *Fragility of Goodness*, 328–29.

14. Nussbaum, *Fragility of Goodness*, 333. I mention Roche here, with an inclusive interpretation mentioned only in a footnote in his paper: "Aristotle would claim that Priam was deprived of happiness through the loss of important external goods and not because he was no longer capable of exercising virtue" (Roche, "Happiness and External Goods," 56n43).

15. For a detailed presentation of Cashen's interpretation of the relationship of external goods and happiness, see chapter 3.

16. Cashen, "Ugly, the Lonely, and the Lowly," 11–13.

action, and (b) happiness is marred because of the inflicted suffering and disappointment.[17]

These two scholars represent the established interpretations of inclusivism and monism, and their explanations show both the common ground of acknowledging the impact of the loss of external goods in terms of diminishing virtuous action, but also the difference in that the monist interpreter will focus on how suffering affects happiness, in contrast with the inclusivist interpreter who focuses on how the loss of sphere of activity affects something deeper than the contended feeling. On a general note, the case of Priam receives little attention from the monist interpreters; see for example, Brown who not even mentions Priam. I understand this little interest on the monist side of the debate in relation to Priam, because the loss of the external goods is interpreted mainly as an impediment towards virtue; the means to do well are gone, and suffering and frustration are blocking happiness in human life; nothing else happens.

I positioned myself mainly on the inclusivist track by focusing both on the instrumental and constitutive roles of external goods in relation to happiness in *EN* (see chapter 5.3–4). Priam's possessions, position, and life are lost in extremely bad circumstances. Because of this, the impact upon his happiness is severe, and I explain the severity of the impact by making reference to the self-sufficiency of happiness. Aristotle understands happiness, the ultimate end of man, as being self-sufficient. For Aristotle, the self-sufficiency of happiness is a relational transformative concept (see the argument in chapter 4). Happiness is self-sufficient, that is, it has everything it needs, because it is an actualizing virtuous activity exercised among others, especially in the city. The self-sufficiency of happiness is founded on the self-sufficiency of the city. But, when the family, friends, and the city are lost, the self-sufficiency of happiness is drastically impacted, it is practically destroyed. Only the character is left.[18] That is why, Priam will not do any bad thing, but will endure with patience everything that happens to him.

One of the most painful moments for Priam misfortunes is the day in which Achilles kills three of his sons: Polydorus, Lycaon, and Hector (*Iliad* 22). The son Hector is mentioned by Aristotle saying that Hector "was very good" (*EN* VII.1, 1145a21, Ross and Urmson). That is why, the death of a

---

17. Cashen, "Ugly, the Lonely, and the Lowly," 12, 17.

18. See also Nussbaum, who says that "calamity does not impair the quality of Priam's life, since he has displayed good character in action consistently through the course of a long life" (Nussbaum, *Fragility of Goodness*, 329).

good son[19] makes his father less likely to be happy. This death of a good son affects the happiness of his father in a very deep way, I argue, it affects its self-sufficiency. By losing Hector, Priam no longer has the possibility of exercising the virtue of a noble father. But the impact is deeper than that: by losing Hector, Priam is no longer happy, but broken in his soul, because the relationship, good son–good father, is severed in a definitive way by death. Priam is still a good person, because his character shines through the worst disaster, and this is seen when he goes to Achilles and begs for the humiliated dead body of Hector to be returned (he even kisses the hand that killed his son). Achilles returns the body of Hector, and Priam can fulfill the duty of a good father to bury and mourn his son (*Iliad* 24).

This drastic impact upon the self-sufficiency of happiness is not definitive. It can be reversed. What is needed is time, high distinctions, and achievements. These are the components needed for rebuilding a happy life: living in a good family, surrounded by friends, in a city (this recovery did not apply to Priam, because, after he has lost everything, he himself is killed[20] on the altar of Zeus by Neoptolemus, the son of Achilles).

These severe misfortunes endured by Priam are relevant for understanding the relationship between happiness and external goods. This is what I will inquire in the next section.

7.4 THE RELEVANCE OF PRIAM'S MISFORTUNES

Such a situation, like that of Priam, does not happen to everyone. There are not many happy people in history who have lost absolutely everything.[21] I interpret the reference to Priam's misfortunes as a reference to something exceptionally bad, the worst test case. My understanding of how Priam's example functions for Aristotle is close to that of Nussbaum, who says that "the story of Priam is a good test case for Aristotle's ethical theory."[22] It is a test case, but I see it as the *worst* test case; in this way, Aristotle makes

---

19. On the virtue of Hector, see Henry, "Aristotle's Best Life," 191–92.

20. Burger observes that at old age happiness is especially "vulnerable because there is no chance to recover from what might have otherwise been only a temporary phase of misery" (Burger, *Aristotle's Dialogue with Socrates*, 38).

21. See also, Emilsson who says that "'happy' can be truly predicated of virtuous people of some means in the middle of their lives but only on condition that their external fortune does not drastically turn against them. Thanks to the stability and resourcefulness of virtue, this rarely happens but it may" (Emilsson, "On Happiness and Time," 227).

22. Nussbaum, *Fragility of Goodness*, 328.

sure that his theory is able to accommodate even the most extreme situations. Thus, Aristotle's point in making reference to Priam's misfortunes is to show how his theory of happiness works even in the most severe aristocratic circumstances.

Suffering, loses, and death are great challenges to any theory of happiness, and they need to be addressed. Priam's misfortunes function as the worst test case where a theory is tested to see how it accommodates the worst possible aristocratic scenario. As I have argued in chapters 2 and 4, Aristotle's theory of happiness includes external goods or some prosperity.

My thesis is that, the relational self-sufficiency of Aristotelian's happiness depends on them. Because of this, Aristotle's theory of happiness is vulnerable.[23] Happiness is not pleasure, wealth, or fame, also is not virtue (*EN* I.4–5), but it is an actualizing virtuous activity of the soul (ψυχῆς ἐνέργεια κατ ἀρετήν, *EN* I.7, 1098a17). Thus, activity, character, and mean are what happiness is, according to Aristotle. Happiness is a complex actualizing virtuous activity. The human necessities of reason and society are built in into what a human is, according to Aristotle: a man is a rational and a political living thing (*EN* IX.9).

Also, the aristocratic flavor is built in how Aristotle understands the role of the external goods. This aspect is clearly seen in *EN* I.8, 1099b1–7. The relationships and contrasts between good birth and good children, and low birth and bad children are at its core. Prestige, discipline, and education is what distinguishes the good man from the irrational, rogue, and envious man of low birth with bad children.[24] The good man of good birth will not end up doing utterly bad actions. The external goods mentioned by Aristotle in *EN* I.8 can be destroyed mainly by death.

This is where the extreme aristocratic case of Priam comes in. Priam was the last king of Troy, a good, wise, and happy man who had all these external goods: good birth, good children, and good friends. When Priam has lost his family, his friends, his wealth, and his political power, his blessedness was marred; by this I mean his pleasurable and joyful life is gone.

---

23. See also Roche's point about the vulnerability of happiness: "Priam's fate brings home the point that happiness for any human being, even a mighty king, is vulnerable to chance and ill fortune" (Roche, "Happiness and External Goods," 56).

24. Halim makes a similar observation when he says that "excellent practical activity for Aristotle thus fails to be equally accessible to all humans both because of its restriction in its fullest form to those with fully rational souls (free adult men), and also because of the circumstantial conditions required for its exercise (wealth, etc.)" (Halim, "Aristotle's Explanation," 184).

When his good children and good friends have died, he was no longer called happy by anyone.

Why? Both on (1) instrumental and (2) intrinsic reasons. (1) He was no longer able to practice his virtues of being a good father and a good king. His children and his city are gone. Being childless and without a kingdom, the two of his main instruments of virtue, being a father and a king, are gone, thus no longer able to practice virtues. Also, his pain and suffering, because of this extreme loses, are deep and they overwhelm his entire life. (2) The intrinsic activity of happiness is profoundly disturbed by these loses. The death of his very good son Hector, and the destruction of his city Troy, destroy his happiness. This is so, because the self-sufficiency of his happiness, which depends on this relational foundation of family and city, is destroyed by death and defeat.

This explanation of why Priam was no longer called happy by others differs from that of others who interpret external goods in inclusivist terms. For example, Russell (an inclusivist scholar) explains the case of Priam as a problem, which in the end, Aristotle cannot say much about it. For Russell, Aristotle cannot call Priam happy, but also, he cannot call Priam unhappy either.[25] The reason for this, according to Russell, is twofold: (1) no virtuous person can ever become wretched, and (2) a person like Priam cannot be called happy by anyone. Thus, Russell says, "Aristotle remains perplexed about cases of virtue faced with serious bad luck."[26] The main thing about Priam's situation, according to Russell, is not so much that he has lost a life of particular activities, but the fact that he was dramatically unlucky.[27] Thus, the fact of Priam's extremely bad luck is how Russell clearly distinguishes himself from an instrumental/constitutive explanation of the reasons for which others would not call Priam happy.

My instrumental/constitutive interpretation acknowledges the magnanimity of the loss suffered by Priam, but it does not focus on the very bad luck suffered by Priam, but on the comprehensiveness of his losses as the complex reason for which others would no longer call Priam happy. The focus on the comprehensive character of Priam's loss, and not on his extremely bad luck, reflects better the textual evidence from *EN* I.10 mentioned by me above. I argue that the point of mentioning Priam is not on how extremely unlucky he was and how perplexed we are, but on how much

---

25. Russell, *Happiness for Humans*, 109.
26. Russell, *Happiness for Humans*, 109.
27. Russell, *Happiness for Humans*, 115.

he has lost. Also, my interpretation of how the meaning of self-sufficiency of happiness is relevant here enhances the understanding of Priam's case by showing that, when he has lost his family and his city, he has lost his happiness, because its self-sufficiency is gone. His character is still there, but his blessedness is marred; as Aristotle says, Priam is no longer supremely blessed (*EN* I.10, 1101a7, Rackham).

7.5 CONCLUSION

Thus, in this chapter I have argued based on the textual evidence from *EN* I.9–10 that what happened to Priam functions as the worst test case against to test a theory of happiness. Aristotle tests his theory of happiness by facing the comprehensive loss of everything: family, friends, wealth, power, and the city.

The result of this test is that (1) the traits of virtuous character of the happy man are strong and not easily to be dislodged, and in adversity the nobility of character shines through, and (2) his happiness is vulnerable, because its self-sufficiency being based on his relationships of family, friends and on the self-sufficiency of the city, is destroyed when the family and friends die, and the city is destroyed. Priam loses more than his sphere of virtuous activity when his family and city are lost, he loses his happiness because its self-sufficiency is destroyed.

CHAPTER 8

AN ANTHROPOLOGICAL DEPENDENCY

8.1 INTRODUCTION

IN *EN* X.8 ARISTOTLE continues to explore the topic of happiness and external goods. This time he seems to be focusing on something different from the previous mentions where the dependency of happiness was conceived in enhancing-instrumental terms and constitutive terms. This time the focus seems to be somewhere else. This is what Aristotle say in *EN* X.8:

> But (1) happiness will need external prosperity also, (2) since we are human beings [ἀνθρώπῳ ὄντι]; (3) for our nature [ἡ φύσις] is not self-sufficient for study, but (4) we need a healthy body, and (5) need to have food and (6) the other services provided. Still, (7) even though no one can be blessedly happy without external goods, (8) we must not think that to be happy we will need many large goods. For (9) self-sufficiency and action do not depend on excess. (*EN* X.8, 1178b32–1179a2, Irwin)

This time, I argue, Aristotle explains happiness's need for external goods not as instruments for virtuous activity, or as constituents of virtuous activity, but in anthropological terms. Aristotle says that happiness needs external goods because we are human beings. This distinctiveness of what Aristotle says here is the fact that made me to treat this dependency in a separate chapter. Even though this text does not have prominence in the scholarly studies on external goods in *EN*, I will interact with whatever various interpreters say about its meaning as my topic is concerned. I will argue that here, Aristotle gives the reader another type of dependency of happiness on external goods, and this time it is an anthropological dependency, or a subsistent dependency. The dependency Aristotle speaks about here is related to the anthropological side of his inquiry. The reason for which in *EN* X.8 the dependency of happiness on external goods is mainly anthropological is that, I argue, happiness is explained as contemplation. Of special interest is Aristotle's statement from *EN* X.8: "Whereas the happiness that belongs to the intellect is separate" (*EN* X.8, 1178a22, Rackham). The meaning of being "separate" needs to be explained carefully because it can help to better understand the dependency of contemplation upon external prosperity.

The structure of this chapter has two main sections: (1) happiness of the intellect (as separable), and (2) happiness/contemplation's anthropological dependency on external goods.

8.2 HAPPINESS OF THE INTELLECT

In chapter 2.2.5 I have offered an overview of Aristotle's inquiry on contemplation. Nonetheless, because there are so many issues regarding how to interpret *EN* X.6–8 as part of Aristotle's study on happiness, I will give my understanding of what I consider to be important in explaining the meaning of contemplation with relevance for it's dependency on external bodily goods. This section is organized in several subsections: (1) complete happiness, (2) activity of the highest part in us, and (3) intellect as separable.

8.2.1 Complete Happiness

The last part of Aristotle's inquiry about εὐδαιμονία in *EN* X.6–7 starts by focusing on the unity of his inquiry.[1] By focusing on the unity of his endeavor, he gives the reader a summary of what he had said so far,

---

1. Also Richardson Lear who says that there are two main reasons for treating the argument about εὐδαιμονία as a unity: (1) there is substantive common ground between Book I and X, and (2) it is the same in *Eudemian Ethics*, Book I, II, and VII, where the focus on virtues and contemplation is peculiar to Aristotle. See Richardson Lear, "Happiness," 401.

and this summary is described by him as an "outline of happiness" (*EN* X.6, 1176a30). This summary shows the major features of the "outline of happiness."

According to Aristotle, εὐδαιμονία, as the aim of human life, has to be classed as ἐνέργειαν τινα (*EN* X.6, 1176b1). This phrase is usually translated as "some form of activity" (Rackham), "in the class of activities" (Crisp), "a sort of activity" (Reeve), or "a certain activity" (Bartlett and Collins). This reference to εὐδαιμονία as ἐνεργεία makes the connection to the previous definition of εὐδαιμονία in I.7. There, as here, happiness is described as "activity" [ἐνεργεία].[2]

This activity is an activity desired for what it is in itself (*EN* X.6, 1177a2), an activity that has everything, that is self-sufficient (*EN* X.6, 1176b5). It is not an activity serving as a means to something else, but it is an end itself (*EN* X.6, 1176b7). As in I.7, this activity is virtuous (*EN* X.6, 1176a10). Aristotle's summary from X.6 confirms my overall formative interpretation of εὐδαιμονία because he says that everything so far in *EN* was a discussion about happiness and virtue in their various "forms" [τύποις] (*EN* X.9, 1179a35). Aristotle's approach to εὐδαιμονία is to be seen as an educational formative process. Aristotle's study is intended as a transformative study/endeavor (see especially chapter 4).

After the review of the "outline of happiness" (*EN* X.6, 1176a31–1177a10) is done, Aristotle makes an important move in advancing his inquiry. He says: "if happiness consists in activity in accordance with virtue, it is reasonable that it should be the activity in accordance with the highest virtue; and this will be the virtue of the best part of us" (*EN* X.7, 1177a12). So, he builds on his previous findings and advances upwards:[3] now he focuses on the "highest virtue" of ἐνεργεία. That is why, what he does in X.6 is not a new account of happiness, but a completion of the previous one, from the Books I and II.

This upward inquiry has a challenge: the best part of us is the intellect, and the intellect, according to Aristotle, is divine (*EN* X.7, 1177b30); and this makes it superior to the human side of our composite nature. The way Aristotle keeps his inquiry together is by saying that these two lives, "the

---

2. Against Van Cleemput who argues for "one [happy] life, but two different activities" (Van Cleemput, "Aristotle on Happiness," 95).

3. Against Shields, who argues that in *EN* Aristotle seems to move from an encompassing understanding of the human good to a narrow understanding of it consisting in contemplation. These two conceptions of the good are not coherent. See Shields, *Aristotle*, 341.

life of the intellect" and "the life of moral virtue" are two stages/degrees available to humans (*EN* X.8, 1178a10). He will continue to apply the main criterion of the "function of man" as this is said explicitly in *EN* X.7, 1178a7: "That which is best and most pleasant for each creature is that which is proper to the nature of each." This underlines the unity of his inquiry but here it reaches the ultimate climax.

Thus, in *EN* X.6–8, Aristotle's inquiry on the good of man is reaching its end. When someone gets closer in reaching its end, his or her life is blessed "in so far as it contains some likeness to the divine activity" (*EN* X.8, 1178b27).[4] In this framework I interpret the phrase "complete happiness" (*EN* X.7, 1177a17; X.8, 1178b7) as happiness reaching its completion.

Aristotle is very careful not to use the phrase "secondary happiness" as some scholars do.[5] "Secondary happiness" is usually understood by these scholars as referring to a distinct kind of life, a virtuous life distinct from a divine life. They work with this distinction between "virtuous human life" and "divine life." I argue that Aristotle speaks here about different stages in people's lives as they strive towards "complete happiness." It is like a singer who, through practice and competition, finally achieves his/her goal of winning a major award or being able to interpret well a major work of music. S/he achieved mastery in that field of work. Aristotle's exact words in *EN* X.8, 1078a10 are: "in a secondary degree, on the other hand, that according to the other virtue" [Δευτέρως δ' ὁ κατὰ τὴν ἄλλην ἀρετήν]. The immediate context of *EN* X.7, 1078a9 speaks about the "life that is happiest," not a "different happy life." The meaning of δευτέρως in *EN* X.8, 1078a10 is related to a degree, not to a distinct kind of life. Aristotle's "happiness as the activity of the soul according to virtue" is not a "secondary happiness" but a stage secondary to last that can be completed in "complete happiness."

So, happiness is the activity according virtue (this is "the other virtue" in *EN* X.8, 1078a10, Ross*). This was the result of Aristotle's inquiry up to *EN* X.6 and, now he develops his thesis by exploring it according to "the highest virtue." This shows that Aristotle works with a hierarchical structure

---

4. Long says that "the gods are the paradigms of happiness" (Long, "Aristotle on *Eudaimonia*," 111). See also Kraut, *Aristotle on the Human Good*, 325. There is a passing mention about the larger metaphysical framework by Roochnik when he says that "theoretical activity actualizes what is most divine in us" (Roochnik, "What is *Theoria*?," 69), but he does not elaborate as his work is only a prolegomenon to a study of θεωρία.

5. See Hardie, "Final Good in Aristotle's Ethics," 279, 282; "Aristotle on the Best Life," 48; Shea, "Happiness and Theorizing," 83; Majithia, "Aristotle on the Good Life," 8; Van Cleemput, "Aristotle on Happiness," 131; Kraut, *Aristotle on the Human Good*, 322–23.

of virtues that allows him to go higher in his inquiry; the higher the part of us, the higher its virtue. Also, the concept of τέλος/aim, end makes him to go all the way up to the end with his inquiry. This is how continuity with the initial definition of εὐδαιμονία (activity/actuality of the soul according to virtue) and its completion (now Aristotle speaks about "complete happiness"), has to be understood: the activity according to (the other) virtue, and the activity according to highest virtue. There is continuity between "activity of the soul according to virtue" and the "activity in accordance with the highest virtue," which is the virtue of "the best part of us."

Thus, there are not two kinds of happiness, one that is "primary" and the other that is "secondary"; Aristotle does not have two accounts of εὐδαιμονία, but one.[6] In Aristotle's *EN*, there is "happiness" and "complete happiness" or the good of man and the good of man reaching its end.[7] Not everyone reaches this end, but only those who are living/working according to their highest virtue.[8]

So far, in this section I argued that Aristotle's inquiry about happiness, started in Book I and II, is reaching its completion in Book X.6. Accordingly, εὐδαιμονία continues to be, for Aristotle in *EN*, the activity, but now he explores this by focusing on the highest virtue, which is the virtue of the highest part of us, the intellect. The intellect is the divine part of us and, that is why, its activity will be the closest we can get to the "pure activity" which is god. The activity of the intellect, contemplation, resembles the activity of the gods. This is "complete happiness," εὐδαιμονία reaching its completion. What I need to do next is to explore the meaning of contemplation as the activity in accordance with the highest virtue.

8.2.2 Activity of the Highest Part

In this subsection I will study the last segment of Aristotle's inquiry: ἐνέργεια in accordance with the highest virtue. The highest virtue is the virtue of the highest part of us, which is the intellect [νοῦς]. First, I will explain how we

---

6. Against Curzer, who says that the criteria used by Aristotle's inquiry about εὐδαιμονία in *EN* X.6–8 and I.7 are very different (Curzer, "Criteria for Happiness," 422). Richardson Lear argues for one account of εὐδαιμονία in *EN* and says that the moral action "approximates" contemplation (Richardson Lear, *Happy Lives*, 177).

7. Also, Majithia who argues that "the good life for the virtuous man is the life of practical virtue ending in contemplation" (Majithia, "Aristotle on the Good Life," 8).

8. Also Pakaluk, who says that "happiness in Aristotelian scheme is meant to be an ideal not a catch-all for people" (Pakaluk, *Aristotle's Nicomachean Ethics*, 322).

need to understand the intellect as an element of the soul, and, second, how we need to understand contemplation [θεώρια] both as "study" and "contemplation." I will argue that the ultimate teleological end of man is the activity [ἐνεργεία] of the mind/intellect [νοῦς], and because the νοῦς, according to Aristotle, is an element of every human soul, this activity is a possibility for every human being.

8.2.2.1 Intellect as an Element of the Soul

In this subsection I will study the intellect, the highest part of us. I will focus my investigation by giving an overview of how intellect, as the highest part of us, is understood by Aristotle in *EN*, then, what is its role as an element of every human soul, and in the end what does it mean that for Aristotle the intellect is divine. I will argue that for Aristotle, in his ethical and biological (*On the Soul* III.5) inquiry, the separable intellect is the main factor of the soul which constitutes the potentiality which can lead to achieving of actuality in every human life.

In *EN* X. 6–8, Aristotle continues to inquiry into the area of virtues by focusing on the "highest" [κράτιστη] [virtue]; Aristotle searches for the "most excellent" virtue. The way he searches for the most excellent virtue, is by exploring it according to the "function" framework. For him the "most excellent" virtue is the virtue of the "best part" [ἄριστος] of us. This is the virtue "proper to it" (*EN* X.7, 1177a14). Aristotle identifies the "best part of us" as the part that "rules and leads us by nature." That part "has cognizance of what is noble and divine" (*EN* X.7, 1177a15). And this is the mind/intellect [νοῦς].

Thus, the factors of ruling, leading and knowing of the noble and divine are the factors used by Aristotle to identify what is best [ἄριστος]. Also "the best" [ἄριστος], which is the mind/intellect [νοῦς] is "divine" [θεῖον] (*EN* X.7, 1177a15). This is the part of us humans that ultimately helps to reach our aim, which is happiness. Because the mind [νοῦς] is divine we are able to reach our aim; god, according to Aristotle, is the pure actuality. The ἐνεργεία of the mind, which is a human activity, is "the greatest source of happiness" (*EN* X.8, 1178b25). To understand better what Aristotle says about νοῦς in *EN* X.6–8, I need to explore his view on it, as he speaks about it in *EN*.

For Aristotle, νοῦς is found in the soul. In the soul, according to Aristotle, there are three elements: intellect [νοῦς], sensation, and desire.

Through them a human being gains control upon his/her actions and attains truth (*EN* VI.2, 1139a19). Aristotle understands humans as creatures of action, and as such, they are a compound of "desire and intellect" [νοῦς] (*EN* VI.2, 1139b5). The human mind attains truth with the help of several qualities: "technical skill, scientific knowledge, prudence, wisdom, and intelligence" [τέχνη ἐπιστήμη φρόνησις σοφία νοῦς] (*EN* VI.3, 1139b16). From these qualities only the mind [νοῦς] is the quality through which humans can apprehend the "first principles" (*EN* VI.3, 1139b16).

Also, Aristotle understands wisdom [σοφία] as a combination of mind [νοῦς] and knowledge [ἐπιστήμη]. This knowledge, according to Aristotle, is the knowledge of the "most exalted objects" (*EN* VI.7, 1141a20). Through wisdom we have knowledge and intelligence of the "things of the most exalted nature" (*EN* VI.7, 1141b3). Our intelligence [νοῦς] has the ability to "apprehend definitions" (*EN* VI.8, 1142a25; see the extended analysis about this in *EN* VI.11, 1143a25–1143b15). This focus on wisdom (mind and knowledge) and the most exalted things will be resurfacing in *EN* X.8, where the philosopher as a wise man is the happiest person.

In the good man, the intellect [νοῦς] "always chooses for itself that which is best." A good man obeys his intellect (*EN* IX.8, 1169a18), and together with virtue [ἀρετή], the intellect/mind [νοῦς] is the "source of man's higher activities" (*EN* X.6, 1176b19). This is what Aristotle says in *EN* about the intellect [νοῦς] before *EN* X.7. An informed interpretation of the intellect [νοῦς] in X.7 needs to take these aspects into consideration. These details about the νοῦς are rarely mentioned and integrated by scholars who inquire about contemplation (the happiness of *the intellect*) and external goods.

So, according to Aristotle, νοῦς is part of every human soul, not only into some, and the νοῦς is the factor that makes the reaching of actuality possible for every human being. The soul is the main element of continuity in his inquiry between what was said before *EN* X.7 and after that. In *EN* I.7, 1098a16 Aristotle's conclusion is that "the good of man is the active exercise of his soul's faculties in conformity with excellence." Now in *EN* X.7–8 he explores the νοῦς as one of the elements in the soul, because this element has two main features: it rules and leads us and knows what is noble and divine (*EN* X.7, 1177a12). Aristotle has a comprehensive way of expressing this in *EN* VI.11, 1143b10: "Intelligence is both beginning and end" [ἀρχὴ καὶ τέλος νοῦς], which means that "ultimates as well as primary are grasped by intelligence" [τῶν πρώτων ὅρων καὶ τῶν ἐσχάτων νοῦς ἐστὶ]

(*EN* VI.11, 1143b1). These exact quotes are very important because they show how important νοῦς is for Aristotle in relation to the first principles (the beginning) and the ultimate purpose of everything. They are apprehended by the νοῦς. Because of νοῦς this movement towards the ultimate aim [τέλος] is possible.

Also, Aristotle says that "intellect is divine" [θεῖον ὁ νοῦς] (*EN* X.7, 1177b30). This fact is explored by Aristotle by way of a comparison between a life at "the human level" [κατ' ἄνθρωπον] (*EN* X.7, 1177b27) and the "higher life" [βίος κρείττων] (*EN* X.7, 1177b27). This higher life is possible for a human because of the νοῦς, which is divine and superior. Thus, the life of the νοῦς is divine when it is compared with human life (*EN* X.7, 1177b34). Aristotle advises humanity to make sure that they live their lives in accordance with their intellect which is the highest part in them (*EN* X.7, 1177b34). He advises them to keep their intellect in the best condition, and to cultivate it by pursuing rational intellectual activities (*EN* X.8, 1179a24). These actions of "pursuing," "cultivating," and "preserving" the intellect are ways in which every human should relate to his/her νοῦς. According to Aristotle the wise man practices these actions (*EN* X.8, 1179a30). According to him, the wise man is "naturally" the happiest [εὐδαιμονέστατον] person and s/he is most loved by the gods (*EN* X.8, 1179a32). This is the last point in Aristotle's inquiry.

This last point about actuality/activity according to the highest virtue has to be seen, not as a distinct stage, but as the potential aim for everyone; the νοῦς is the most powerful and valuable part a person has (*EN* X.7, 1178a1), and it has the ability to apprehend the first principles and the most exalted things in nature. Thus, with the help of νοῦς, the good/virtuous person can practice "higher activities," and, as I will argue later in the chapter, the external goods in moderation are needed for it.

Now that I have explored the meaning of the intellect and its role in explaining contemplation, I need to explore the meaning of happiness of the intellect as being separable and its implications for my thesis.

8.2.2.2 *Happiness of the Intellect is Separate*

This statement of Aristotle from *EN* X.8 that "the happiness that belongs to the intellect is separate" (*EN* X.8, 1078a22, Rackham) is understood by scholars in connection with *De Anima* III.5. I will study this statement by looking at the various problems it poses for project. First, I will discuss the problems with translating it into English, then, second, I will inquire about the role of *De Anima* III.5 in explaining it,[9] and three, its importance for my study.

It can be seen that various English translations translate it differently: "Whereas the happiness that belongs to the intellect is separate" (Rackham); "but the happiness belonging to the intellect is separate" (Bartlett and Collins); "the excellence of the intellect is a thing apart" (Ross and Urmson); "the virtue of understanding, however, is separated [from the compound]" (Irwin); "the virtue of intellect, however, is separate" (Crisp); and "the virtue of understanding, though, is separated" (Reeve). The reason for these differences is the elliptical style of Aristotle's saying. In Greek, he says, ἡ δὲ τοῦ νοῦ κεχωρισμένη, which can be translated literally into English as "but [that] of the intellect is separate" (my translation). The question is to what from the immediate previous context Aristotle refers here. The scholars are divided here: Rackham and Bartlett and Collins say that it refers to "[happiness] of the intellect," and Ross and Urmson, Irwin, Crisp, and Reeve say that it refers to "[virtue] of the intellect" (see their translations above). The statement Aristotle makes right before it says this: "so therefore also is the life that manifests these virtues, and the happiness that belongs to it" (*EN* X.8, 1078a21). Because "happiness/εὐδαιμονία" is the closest term used previously by Aristotle, it is very likely that this should be assumed when he says "but, [that] of the intellect is separate" as referring to the εὐδαιμονία of the νοῦς. Joachim interprets in a similar way, when he says that "in this latter passage, ἡ δὲ τοῦ νοῦ κεχωρισμένη (*EN* 1178a22) must be interpreted ἡ δὲ τοῦ νοῦ εὐδαιμονία κεχωρισμένη."[10]

If this is the case, what does it mean that the happiness of the intellect is separate? Is separate from what? Reeve explains the meaning of being separable as "separate from the body and from other elements in the soul

---

9. There are other texts that can be relevant for a better understanding of what Aristotle says here in *EN* X.8 1078a22: "Understanding and contemplation are extinguished because something else within passes away, but it itself is unaffected" (Aristotle, *De Anima* I.4 408b18–25); "It remains then that understanding alone enters [the body of the male seed in the process of embryogenesis] additionally from outside and alone is divine, since bodily activity is in no way associated with its activity" (Aristotle, *GA* II.3 736b15–29); "Consider now the body of the seed, in and with which is emitted the starting-point of the soul, part of which is separate from the body and belongs to those beings in which something divine is included (and this is what is called understanding), while the other is not separate from the body" (Aristotle, *GA* II.3 737a7–11). See Reeve, "Notes," 348.

10. Joachim, *Aristotle*, 287.

that are the body's form."[11] Broadie says that this phrase "means minimally, that intelligence can be defined without reference to the body or to non-rational part of the soul."[12] Also, Joachim says that the νοῦς "is independent of, and unaffected by, the bodily conditions."[13]

These various explanations of the meaning of being separate as the intelligence/reason is concerned are based on various understandings of what Aristotle says is *De Anima* III.5, which is probably the most debated text of Aristotle.[14] In *De Anima* III.5, Aristotle makes a distinction between active and passive intellect; the active intellect is separable from the body being unmixed and impassible:

> And this reason is separate and unaffected and unmixed, being in its essence actuality. For what acts is always superior to what is affected, as too the first principle is to the matter. [Knowledge in actuality is the same as the thing, though in an individual knowledge in potentiality is prior in time, though generally it is not prior in time.] But it is not the case that sometimes it reasons and sometimes it does not. And having been separated, this alone is just what it is, and this alone is deathless and everlasting, though we do not remember, because this is unaffected, whereas passive reason is perishable. And without this, nothing reasons. (*De Anima* III.5, 430a17–25, Shields)

The debate concerning the meaning of this text in Aristotle's anthropology is vast and it is not the purpose of this section to enter into it.[15] But this text is relevant for understanding the meaning of being "separate" concerning the happiness of the intellect from *EN* X.8. Thus, according to *De anima* III.5, the intellect, unlike the other faculties of the soul, such as desire, movement, or perception, does not need the body or an organ from the body; also, it is associated with the divine. And in *EN* X.8, 1078a10–21, on the one hand, the moral virtues are related to our bodily nature as they involve passions and have a material aspect. The passions of a human being are accompanied by changes at physical level. And the practical wisdom/prudence (φρόνησις) cannot be separated from moral virtue (*EN* X.8,

---

11. Reeve, "Notes," 347.
12. Broadie, "Book X," 445.
13. Joachim, *Aristotle*, 290.
14. Shields, "Book III," 312.
15. See the latest analysis of it (divine interpretation *versus* human interpretation) in Shields, "Book III," 325–29.

1078a17), and as such ultimately is linked to the body. On the other hand, the theoretical intellect is separate from our bodily nature.[16]

But, specifically, Aristotle mentions in *EN* X.8, 1078a22, that "the happiness of the intellect is separate." Aristotle does not say that the intellect *per se* is separate, but that the happiness of the intellect is separate. The consensus is that, it is separated from our physical constitution. But Aristotle does not give the details of this separatedness. Most likely, the happiness of the intellect is separate from the moral virtue on the basis that it is the happiness of something that is separate in itself from our physical constitution and that is the intellect. Aristotle does not elaborate, he just says that "so much may be said about it here, for a full discussion of the matter is beyond the scope of our present purpose" (*EN* X.8, 1078a23, Rackham). The relevant point for my project is that even the separatedness of the happiness of the intellect from the body, this separatedness is not of such nature that excludes dependency on the bodily goods, such as health. This anthropological dependency is what I explore in the next section.

8.3 CONTEMPLATION'S ANTHROPOLOGICAL DEPENDENCY ON EXTERNAL GOODS

This section explores the anthropological dependency of contemplation on the external goods. I will do this by evaluating the hedonistic interpretation of Cooper, then I will explore the meaning of our humanity and its relevance for explaining the dependency of contemplation on it. I argue that a comprehensive, anthropological understanding of dependency of contemplation makes betters sense of what Aristotle does in this text.

8.3.1 Ordinary Pleasures

Aristotle's reference to happiness and external goods from *EN* X.8, 1178b32–1179a2, is important and addresses the topic I study within the larger context of *EN* X.6–8: happiness as contemplation and its relationship to external goods. Let us read again what Aristotle says here:

> But (1) happiness will need external prosperity also, (2) since we are human beings [ἀνθρώπῳ ὄντι]; (3) for our nature [ἡ φύσις] is not self-sufficient for study, but (4) we need a healthy body, and

---

16. Scott, "Aristotle on the Good Life," 358.

(5) need to have food and (6) the other services provided. Still, (7) even though no one can be blessedly happy without external goods, (8) we must not think that to be happy we will need many large goods. For (9) self-sufficiency and action do not depend on excess. (*EN* X.8, 1178b32–1179a2, Irwin)

The meaning of dependency of happiness on external goods in this text is interpreted by Cooper in the following way. The pleasure of eating, drinking and engaging in daily activities has value; they are themselves necessities of life. If someone, for some reason, does not have these pleasures, that person would lack something valuable.[17] Cooper insists that here Aristotle cannot refer simply to what we need for staying alive, because in the absence of these, life would not be possible. What Aristotle has in view, according to Cooper, are the things life needs even if it can be conducted without them.[18] Cooper's reference to our text is short and without much detail, that is why my engagement with it will be short.

Aristotle says here that happiness needs external prosperity. As I have already said, external prosperity/goods refer to things external to the soul. By saying that Aristotle's main point here is the necessities of life as the pleasures we get from our daily activities (eating, drinking, etc.) is to say, (1) something Aristotle does not say explicitly, and (2) to forget that the happiness of the intellect is separate from the body. The natural reading of the text is by focusing on the reason Aristotle gives the reader: contemplation needs external goods because we are human beings, and by being human beings he means that, our human nature is not self-sufficient for contemplation. Having a healthy body and food to eat, it has value, not because we like to eat and drink, but because (1) life without them is not possible, and (2) our human nature, which is essentially political and composite, is not self-sufficient for contemplation (these externals are needed for being able to study and contemplate).

8.3.2 Human Nature and the External Goods

Aristotle says that, the external goods are needed for contemplation because the nature of man is not self-sufficient. Every human being needs a healthy body, food and other services. Even when the philosopher practices

---

17. Cooper, *Knowledge, Nature, and the Good*, 298.
18. Cooper, *Knowledge, Nature, and the Good*, 297.

θεωρία there is the need for external goods. The reason for that is that his nature/φύσις is not self-sufficient.

To better understand what Aristotle says here about the lack of self-sufficiency of our human nature/φύσις, I need to explore what else he says about φύσις in *EN*. Without being exhaustive, in *EN*,[19] Aristotle makes several important observations about our human nature: (1) it is a political nature (*EN* I.7, 1097b11), and (2) it is a composite nature (body and soul).

To elucidate what Aristotle says here in X.8, I need to make reference to the other text in *EN* where the nature of man and self-sufficiency are used together. That text is *EN* I.7, 1097b7–17. I have studied it in chapter 4; that is why, I will not go in depth here. My interpretation of the self-sufficiency of happiness in *EN* is mainly in relational political terms. The self-sufficiency of happiness depends upon the self-sufficiency of the city. Because of this, happiness on its own is self-sufficient and makes life choiceworthy. The good of man is a political good (it is the good of the science of Politics).

This insight is fundamental for explaining the dependency of happiness on external goods in instrumental (see chapter 5), constitutive (see chapter 6), and anthropological terms. Aristotle's point in *EN* X.8 about the lack of self-sufficiency of happiness needs to be understood in the larger political context of the self-sufficiency of the city, and the self-sufficiency of happiness that is based upon it. What I want to say is this: because our human nature is political, we are beings that depend upon various political arrangements in a particular city. We do not do well by ourselves; we need others to do life together with (family, friends, fellow citizens). And beside this, we need a healthy body and food. These external goods are subsistent goods that make life possible (that is why, they are so valuable). This is the reason for Aristotle saying that our nature lacks self-sufficiency: it needs a city, and especially it needs healthy body, food, and other services. Its lack of self-sufficiency makes the political human nature dependent on a healthy body and food. These goods of the body, health and food, are not instrumental or constitutive of contemplation. Contemplation as the happiness of the intellect does not need them for practicing virtue or to contemplate, but it needs them for staying alive. They are a necessity of life.

---

19. Aristotle's usage of φύσις in *EN* is extensive. See *EN* 1094b16; 1096a21; 1097b11; 1099a12, 13; 1103a19–20, 24, 26; 1106a9, 10; 1112a25; 1113a21; 1114a26; 1114b14, 16; 1133a30; 1134b25, 29–31, 33; 1135a10, 33; 1137b18; 1141b3, 6; 1144b5; 1148a24, 29; 1148b3, 15, 18, 29; 1149a7; 1152a31; 1152b27; 1153a5; 1153b32; 1154b16; 1154b20, 23; 1155a16; 1161a18; 1162a17; 1169b20; 1170a1, 14, 21; 1190b1, 15, 32; 1178a5; 1179b20; 1180b7; cf. *TLG Workplace 7.0*.

Even if the happiness of the intellect is separate from the body, it is not separate in such a way that exists outside of it. Every human being has a body and for living, this body needs to be healthy and nourished with food. Health and food are necessary for happiness because our life depends on them. They are an anthropological necessity, and this fact makes them necessary for a human being to be able to contemplate.

But, as I mentioned before, there is another fact about our human nature that needs to be explored to see if it is relevant to explain our text: our human nature, according to Aristotle, is composite, and this is what we have in *EN* about this aspect of our human nature. In *EN* I.13, Aristotle understands the soul with the help of φύσις when he says that "another nature in the soul [τις φύσις τῆς ψυχῆς] would also seem to be nonrational, though in a way it shares in reason" (*EN* I.13, 1102b17, Irwin). This use of φύσις make reference to the elements in the soul. To the φύσις of the soul belongs rational and non-rational elements. This complexity of the soul, expressed with the help of φύσις, shows how Aristotle understands the nature of the soul. For him, the soul has a composite nature.

But in *EN* VII.13, 1153b32, he says that "for all things by nature have something divine [in them]" [πάντα γὰρ φύσει ἔχει τι θεῖον]. This saying is confirmed later in *EN* X.6, by Aristotle in relation to man, when he says that the highest thing in us, our intellect, is divine. Because of this divine element, all things pursue pleasure (*EN* VII.13, 1153b29). This divine element from our φύσις makes us all search for pleasure. But because our human nature is not simple, but composite (*EN* VII.14, 1154b22) we find ourselves driven in several directions. This is an important difference between humans and god: the humans have a composite nature and god, according to Aristotle, has a simple nature (*EN* VII.14, 1154b26). That is why, the humans cannot enjoy simple pleasure without change, as god does. Our composite human nature leads us to do various actions, some of them are pleasant, but others are not. Whereas god, who has a simple nature, will always be led towards the most pleasant activity (*EN* VII.14, 1154b26). Human beings will try to avoid the painful actions and pursue what is pleasant. And according to Aristotle our human φύσις is what helps us to do this (*EN* VIII.5, 1157b18). These are the main points about φύσις made by Aristotle in *EN* before *EN* X.8, 1178b35, where he says that "our nature is not self-sufficient" for θεωρία.

Thus, based on these insights about φύσις in *EN* until X.8, I need to explain again in what way φύσις is not self-sufficient. Aristotle says that the activity of study or contemplation needs external support like health, food and other services (*EN* X.8 1179a3). It is not that the external goods bring a contribution to θεωρία, but that they sustain the nature of the person who practices the activity of θεωρία. Höffe speaks about this aspect in a somehow similar way: "man owes his happiness not so much to external powers but to himself."[20] No human being can live without external goods like food and health. Because the subject of Aristotle's inquiry is human good/happiness (*EN* I.13, 1102a15) the external goods are a necessity. The human nature is not self-sufficient as happiness is. This distinction between the self-sufficiency of εὐδαιμονία and the lack of self-sufficiency of φύσις has to be preserved.

The "self-sufficiency" of εὐδαιμονία is a political concept as I showed in chapter 4, because only when people establish together a village or a city, they can become self-sufficient. No one by himself is self-sufficient. That is why, Aristotle says that human φύσις is not self-sufficient by itself. The fact that εὐδαιμονία is ultimately a political aim, which means that it is the supreme good lived in the city, its self-sufficiency is guaranteed.

Nonetheless, there is an organic link between the physical aspect of human life and the virtuous aspect, and that is the common human nature. In our φύσις we experience all our life and activities. Thus, the external goods are part of the inquiry about happiness because the human nature is not self-sufficient. This is the fact that has to be part of any debate about the relationship between happiness and external goods.

Then, when Aristotle speaks about the amount of the external goods needed, he is careful. He has to make sure that the "moral conduct" does not depend on "many possessions" (*EN* X.8, 1179a3). Also, the self-sufficiency of our human nature does not "depend on excessive abundance," but, as I shown above, on some basic goods such as food and health. In fact, as Aristotle observes, the inhabitants of the city are more willing to do virtuous actions than the leaders and the powerful individuals in the city. Aristotle says that anyone can do noble deeds without being a ruler; what is needed is moderate resources (*EN* X.8, 1179a5). Thus, the practice of noble deeds depends on the willingness and some resources of the people (*EN* X.8, 1179a9). I have studied the instrumental dependency of happiness on external goods in chapter 5, and that is why I will not focus on it here.

20. Höffe, *Aristotle*, 148.

8.4 CONCLUSION

In this chapter I have argued that, for Aristotle in *EN* X.8, as the happiness of the intellect is concerned, the external goods are needed for sustaining life. The anthropological dependency is part of Aristotle's overall understanding of the dependency of happiness on external goods in *EN*. Because the happiness of the intellect is separate from the body, the interpreter faces new challenges in explaining the relationship between happiness/contemplation and external goods. The activity of study and contemplation faces the challenge of having a non-self-sufficient human nature. Our human nature is not indestructible and not a *perpetuum mobile*. Our human nature depends on a healthy body, on food and on other services.

Thus, the external bodily goods of health and food have an indirect contribution to happiness as sustaining the life of our human nature. With their help contemplation (the happiness of the intellect), which is separate from the body, can take place.

CHAPTER 9

CONCLUSION

THE DEPENDENCY OF HAPPINESS on external goods is complex. In *EN*, these two items are integrated and developed in various ways. This project explored these ways and argues mainly for three types of dependencies used by Aristotle to accommodate his understanding of happiness and external goods. Usually the debates focus on either one or two ways in which happiness depends on external goods (instrumental and constitutive). My interpretation explores these options, refines them politically, and, in relation to happiness as contemplation, adds another type of dependency, subsistent/anthropological, in its relation to external bodily goods.

In *EN*, both happiness and external goods are continuously developed concepts. In relation to happiness, Aristotle, in his inquiry, moves from happiness to complete happiness, and uses several criteria to explore this complex concept: finality, self-sufficiency, and function. Happiness as the ultimate political good and the virtuous activity of the soul is a concept anchored by Aristotle in the personal, social, and practical life of the individual who lives in the city. In this project I have argued that the political self-sufficiency of the ultimate political good, and our political humanity need to be the main perspectives for interpreting the dependency of happiness on external goods.

Happiness is the aim of the ruling science of Politics; the good of man, in *EN*, is understood by Aristotle in political terms. It is the good of the city. This political social understanding of happiness is the foundation for understanding its self-sufficiency. The self-sufficiency of happiness depends on the self-sufficiency of the city. The relational network of every person: his/her family, friends, and the city is the foundation of life. According to Aristotle, every human being, by nature, is political. It is the nature of every person to be with others. This is what everyone is. It is constitutive of our political humanity. Being among and with others is what we are.

Based on this political understanding of the self-sufficiency of the virtuous activity of the soul, and on our political humanity, I argue that (1) happiness depends on external goods in an enhancing instrumental way. To do fine acts, a happy person needs resources, like friends, wealth and political power. My political interpretation of the instrumental dependency of happiness on external goods argues that they are ultimately needed for enhancing the well-being of the city. The individual is part of this large political network and to play a noble part into it, s/he needs friends, wealth, and political power. This is how happiness as a political good is self-sufficient, because it is the hierarchical ultimate good towards which all other intrinsic goods aim. When every fellow-citizen exercises the virtuous activity of his soul, this political network of friends, wealth, and political power comes together and makes the city self-sufficient.

The practice of virtue with the help of external goods is a political enterprise. A noble action needs friends, wealth, and political power. As it strengthens the good of the city, it strengthens the personal good political character. Doing virtuous actions enhances the virtuous character of the happy political person. Good relationships, material resources, and political support are the political equipment, the political good, happiness needs.

(2) Happiness depends on external goods in a constitutive way. My political interpretation of the self-sufficiency of happiness and our political humanity is the foundation for interpreting the dependency of happiness on external goods in a constitutive way. Aristotle's approach in relation to the constitutive dependency is mainly *via negativa*. He explains what happens to happiness as a possibility for a human being when the external goods are absent: it mars it, it makes it difficult, or it makes it almost impossible.

The external goods of good birth, good children, and beauty are ultimately relational/political in value. For Aristotle a good birth implies prestigious ancestry with noble parents who provided a good education for their child. This aristocratic good assumes a prosperous formative background into which good character is formed through education. When all this is absent, blessedness (pleasure and joy) is marred. This external good of good birth focuses on what the family constitutes for a child. What the family is and does in the life of a child becomes part of what that child is. This is an advantage that, when it is absent, it disfigures the blessedness of that child. Something essential is absent, and that is why, the identity of that child is affected.

The other external good mentioned by Aristotle as being absent is good children. This situation may refer to three scenarios: (a) this parent is without children, (b) with children but they are not good, and (c) s/he had good children, but they are no more. I read Aristotle's saying as intentionally ambiguous, it is comprehensive in that it can refer to any of these situations. I argue that the main point is that when a virtuous happy political person does not have good children, according to any of the above scenarios, something constitutive for his political life and nature is missing. We are what we are among and with others, and the closest to us in this relational-social understanding of human nature, is our family, our children.

Having good children is the result of a good formative education. But this outcome is not guaranteed. A parent can do everything in his power to educate his child, and the child in the end may choose not to listen and not to follow the education that s/he has received. When something like this happens, the blessedness of the parent is marred. The joy of the parent is disfigured because his children are not good. This impact upon the blessedness of the parent is not because the parent does not have the opportunity to practice the virtue of parenthood, but because such a parent does not have good children; the relationship with his good child is absent. The good children of a happy parent are not instruments for him to practice the virtue of parenthood, but they are constitutive of his own political nature and, as such, of his own happiness. When they are absent, in whatever way, the fact of absence ruins the blessedness of the parent. Someone is a parent because they have children; someone is a happy parent because they have good children. That is why, when the good children are absent the parent's blessedness is marred.

The beauty of a person refers to different things according to age. A person is beautiful mainly by the symmetry of his physical appearance. At a young age, a person is beautiful due to being prepared to compete at various games, at adult age, a person is beautiful by being ready for war, and at old age, a person is beautiful if s/he is able to move around and not depend on others. Thus, according to Aristotle, beauty is based on the symmetry of the body and of how well that person faces the challenges of life. When such an item is absent, blessedness is marred. Beauty, ultimately, is a relational constitutive good. We are beautiful for ourselves and for others. That is why, when beauty is absent, our political nature is affected and also our political good, happiness.

Beauty is not mainly an instrument for sexual fulfillment or for being appreciated by others. Beauty is part of what a person is. We speak about someone as being beautiful, and by that we do not primarily mean that his/her beauty will help with finding various sexual partners. Being beautiful is part of the ideal life of a person. It does not diminish with age as physical beauty does, but it evolves with age. It continues to be part of what someone is. That is why, when the beauty, understood as such, is absent, the blessedness is ruined. The major things meant by beauty at various ages are ultimately political. A young athlete who wins various competitions will ultimately bring honor to his/her city, an adult victorious warrior has fought in war for the protection and well-being of his/her city, and an old person is able to take care of himself and not being a burden on anyone in his family.

The scenario of someone being utterly ugly, of low birth, of being childless, and alone is interpreted according to the constitutive understanding of happiness's dependency on the external goods as not making happiness possible. These are various scenarios in which some constitutive features of personal political identity make happiness an impossibility.

The ugliness of a person is understood by Aristotle as having a moral foundation. Aristotle chooses to use a term that is rare but known for expressing extremely shameful acts (such as lying when under oath). These utterly ugly acts make someone utterly ugly as a person. For such an individual happiness is not possible because most likely his/her character and acts are shameful and his/her appearance is mean. When someone is utterly ugly in his deeds, deeds that reflect his character and ultimately his appearance, happiness is a very unlikely possibility. Being utterly ugly is constitutive of what someone is, and this is the reason for which happiness is not possible. It is not that happiness is not a possibility because that utterly ugly person does not have the instruments to practice virtue (such a person may very well be rich and powerful). Such a person cannot be happy because s/he is utterly ugly in actions and appearance. Such a person is bad.

Being born in a poor family, according to Aristotle, means low status in the life of the city; it means a low or weak political nature. In such a situation of poverty and weakness it is difficult to guide life according to reason. From such a social condition of poverty, degradation happens. Such people end up envying those who have more than them or are better than them.

The lack of rational principle, and the presence of envy and roguery, makes happiness hardly possible. The political nature of such a person has turned bad or is weak, and as such, the political good is hardly possible.

When a human being lives is solitude, that person, because s/he lacks relationships, very likely will end up unhappy. This is so because, for Aristotle, the self-sufficient ultimate political good is possible in the context of strong relationships in the city. It is similar with being childless. When a man and his wife do not have children, Aristotle says, their bond is not strong. Being childless leads to weak relationships, because the children are the bond of a strong union between man and his wife, and this makes happiness hardly a possibility.

Next, Aristotle present two very difficult scenarios of having utterly bad children/friends, and having good children/friends who have died, and say, that these pose the greatest problem for happiness; when these things happen, happiness is a very distant possibility. I interpret these scenarios and their relevance for happiness by focusing on two facts. (A) The fact that someone has utterly bad children or friends is, in some measure, a reflection of his/her own character. There is a measure of reciprocal character formation, which is based on Aristotle's understanding of our human nature as being a political nature. (B) When someone's good children or friends die, happiness is very unlikely because the relationships between good parents/friends and their children/friends is a reciprocal profound virtuous political relationship. This reciprocal virtuous political relationship makes happiness possible. When death happens, this reciprocal virtuous political relationship is destroyed, and happiness as a political good is a very distant possibility.

Such losses are found in the case of King Priam. Aristotle tests his theory of happiness against one of the worst known scenarios. Suffering, losses, and death are great challenges for any theory of happiness, and they need to be addressed. Because Aristotle's theory of happiness includes external goods, happiness according to him, is vulnerable to fortune. The human necessities of reason and society are built in into what a human is, and as such, happiness is, according to Aristotle, a complex actualizing virtuous political activity. When a person loses everything, family, friends, political power, and ultimately his/her city, what happens to his/her happiness? When Priam has lost everything, he has lost his happiness, because the political self-sufficiency of happiness is gone, and his political humanity is dismantled. His character is still there, but his blessedness is marred, and his happiness, in those conditions, is not possible.

(3) The last aspect of the dependency of happiness addressed by Aristotle is the dependency of the happiness of intellect on external goods (*EN* X.8). For Aristotle, happiness of the intellect is a thing apart from the body, but not in a way that it is outside the body. Because we are human beings, external bodily goods are still necessary. We need a healthy body, food, and other services, as our human nature is not indestructible and not a *perpetuum mobile*. This is a subsistent dependency, as our life depends on having a healthy body, food, and other services. Contemplation, the happiness of the intellect, needs these basics conditions of life.

BIBLIOGRAPHY

Ackrill, J. L. "Aristotle on *Eudaimonia.*" In *Aristotle's Ethics: Critical Essays*, edited by N. Sherman, 57–78. Lanham, MD: Rowman & Littlefield, 1999.
Almeida, Joseph A. "Gabriel Richardson Lear, *Happy Lives and the Highest Good: An Essay on Aristotle's Nicomachean Ethics.*" *Bryn Mawr Classical Review* 2.51 (2004). http://bmcr.brynmawr.edu/2004/2004-06-46.html.
Altobello, Robert J. "Five Ancient Theories of Happiness." PhD diss., City University of New York, 1997.
Anagnostopoulos, Georgios. *Aristotle on the Goals and Exactness of Ethics*. Berkeley: University of California Press, 1994.
Annas, Julia. "Aristotle on Virtue and Happiness." In *Aristotle's Ethics: Critical Essays*, edited by N. Sherman, 35–56. Lanham, MD: Rowman & Littlefield, 1999.
———. *The Morality of Happiness*. Oxford: Oxford University Press, 1993.
Apostle, Hippocrates G., trans. *Aristotle, The Nicomachean Ethics*. Dordrecht: D. Reidel, 1975.
Aquinas, Thomas. *Commentary on the Nicomachean Ethics*. Translated by C. I. Litzinger. Chicago: Henry Regnery, 1964.
Aristotle. *Athenian Constitution*. Translated by H. Rackham. Cambridge, MA: Harvard University Press, 1952.
———. *De Anima*. Translated by Christopher Shields. Clarendon Aristotle Series. Oxford: Clarendon, 2016.
———. "Nicomachean Ethics." In *The Complete Works of Aristotle: The Revised Oxford Translation*, edited by Jonathan Barnes, 1729–1867. Translated by W. D. Ross. Revised by J. O. Urmson. Vol. 2. Princeton: Princeton University Press, 1984.
———. *Nicomachean Ethics*. Translated by Robert C. Bartlett and Susan D. Collins. Chicago: University of Chicago Press, 2011.
———. *Nicomachean Ethics*. Translated and edited by Roger Crisp. Cambridge Texts in the History of Philosophy. Cambridge: Cambridge University Press, 2004.
———. *Nicomachean Ethics*. Translated by Terrence Irwin. 2nd edition. Indianapolis: Hackett, 1999.
———. *Nicomachean Ethics*. Translated by H. Rackham. Cambridge, MA: Harvard University Press, 1934.
———. *Nicomachean Ethics*. Translated with an introduction and notes by C. D. C. Reeve. Indianapolis: Hackett, 2014.
———. *Nicomachean Ethics*. Translated by W. D. Ross. Oxford: Clarendon, 1908.

BIBLIOGRAPHY

———. *Nicomachean Ethics*. Translated by Christopher Rowe. Edited by Sarah Broadie and Christopher Rowe. Oxford: Oxford University Press, 2002.

———. "Politics." In *The Complete Works of Aristotle: The Revised Oxford Translation*, edited by Jonathan Barnes, 1986–2129. Translated by B. Jowett. Vol. 2. Princeton: Princeton University Press, 1984.

———. "Rhetoric." In *The Complete Works of Aristotle: The Revised Oxford Translation*, edited by Jonathan Barnes, 2152–2269. Translated by W. Rhys Roberts. Vol. 2. Princeton: Princeton University Press, 1984.

Arnn, Kathleen. "Happiness and the Political Life: Aristotle's Treatment of Magnanimity, Justice, and Prudence." PhD diss., Claremont Graduate University, 2013.

Aspasius. *On Aristotle Nicomachean Ethics 1–4, 7–8*. Translated by David Konstan. London: Bloomsbury, 2006.

Baracchi, Claudia. *Aristotle's Ethics as First Philosophy*. Cambridge: Cambridge University Press, 2007.

Broadie, Sarah. "Book I." In *Nicomachean Ethics*, edited by Sarah Broadie and Christopher Rowe, 261–94. Oxford: Oxford University Press, 2002.

———. "Book X." In *Nicomachean Ethics*, edited by Sarah Broadie and Christopher Rowe, 429–52. Oxford: Oxford University Press, 2002.

———. *Ethics with Aristotle*. New York: Oxford University Press, 1991.

Brown, Eric. "Wishing for Fortune, Choosing Activity: Aristotle on External Goods and Happiness." In *Proceedings of the Boston Area Colloquium in Ancient Philosophy*, edited by John J. Cleary and Gary M. Gurtler, 57–81. Leiden: Brill, 2006.

Burger, Ronna. *Aristotle's Dialogue with Socrates on the Nicomachean Ethics*. Chicago: University of Chicago Press, 2008.

Bury, R. G., trans. *Plato in Twelve Volumes*. 12 vols. London: William Heinemann, 1967.

Bush, Stephen S. "Divine and Human Happiness in *Nicomachean Ethics*." *The Philosophical Review* 117.1 (2008) 49–75.

Caesar, I. "Why We Should Not Be Unhappy About Happiness Via Aristotle: The Functionalist Account of Aristotle's Notion of *Eudaimonia*." PhD diss., City University of New York, 2009.

Cashen, Matthew. "The Ugly, the Lonely, and the Lowly: Aristotle on Happiness and the External Goods." *History of Philosophy Quarterly* 29.1 (2012) 1–19.

Collins, Susan D. "The Ends of Action: The Moral Virtues in Aristotle's *Nicomachean Ethics*." PhD diss., Boston College, 1994.

———. "Moral Virtue and the Limits of the Political Community in Aristotle's Nicomachean Ethics." *American Journal of Political Science* 48.1 (2004) 46–61.

Cooper, John. "Aristotle on the Goods of Fortune." *The Philosophical Review* 94.2 (1985) 173–96.

———. *Knowledge, Nature, and the Good: Essays on Ancient Philosophy*. Princeton: Princeton University Press, 2004

———. *Reason and Emotion: Essays on Ancient Moral Psychology and Ethical Theory*. Princeton: Princeton University Press, 1999.

Crisp, Roger. "Introduction." In *Nicomachean Ethics*, edited by Roger Crisp, vii–xxxv. Translated by Roger Crisp. Cambridge Texts in the History of Philosophy. Cambridge: Cambridge University Press, 2004.

Curzer, Howard J. *Aristotle & Virtues*. Oxford: Oxford University Press, 2012.

———. "Criteria for Happiness in *Nicomachean Ethics* I.7 and X.6–8." *The Classical Quarterly* 40.2 (1990) 421–32.

BIBLIOGRAPHY

DeWitt, Norman, trans. *Demosthenes*. Cambridge, MA: Harvard University Press, 1949.

Donoghue-Armstrong, Elizabeth. "Teleology, Perfectionism, and Communitarianism in Aristotle's Political Naturalism." PhD diss., University of Colorado, 2004.

Emilsson, E. K. "On Happiness and Time." In *The Quest for the Good Life: Ancient Philosophers on Happiness*, edited by Oyvind Rabbas, et al., 222–40. Oxford: Oxford University Press, 2015.

Fossheim, Hallvard. "Aristotle on Happiness and Old Age." In *The Quest for the Good Life: Ancient Philosophers on Happiness*, edited by Oyvind Rabbas, et al., 113–26. Oxford: Oxford University Press, 2015.

Fowler, Harold North, trans. *Plato*. Cambridge, MA: Harvard University Press, 1925.

Gomez-Lobo, Alfonso. "The Ergon Inference." *Phronesis* 34.2 (1989) 170–84.

Groarke, Louis F. "Aristotle: Logic." Internet Encyclopedia of Philosophy. http://www.iep.utm.edu/aris-log/#H12.

Halim, I. "Aristotle's Explanation for the Value of the External Goods." PhD diss., Columbia University, 2012.

Hardie, W. F. R. "Aristotle on the Best Life for a Man." *Philosophy* 54.207 (1979) 35–50.

———. "The Final Good in Aristotle's Ethics." *Philosophy* 40.154 (1965) 277–95.

Heinaman, R. "*Eudaimonia* and Self-Sufficiency in the Nicomachean Ethics." *Phronesis* 33.1 (1988) 31–53.

Henry, Darryl I. "Aristotle's Best Life: An Examination of Human Nature." PhD diss., Claremont Graduate University, 2009.

Hester, Marcus. "Aristotle on the Function of Man in Relation to *Eudaimonia*." *History of Philosophy Quarterly* 8.1 (1991) 3–14.

Höffe, Otfried. *Aristotle*. Albany: State University of New York, 2003.

Hughes, Gerard J. *The Routlege Guidebook to Aristotle's Nicomachean Ethics*. London and New York: Routledge, 2013.

Irwin, Terrence. "Conceptions of Happiness in the Nicomachean Ethics." In *The Oxford Handbook of Aristotle*, edited by Christopher Shields, 495–524. Oxford: Oxford University Press, 2012.

———. "Permanent Happiness: Aristotle and Solon." In *Aristotle's Ethics: Critical Essays*, edited by Nancy Sherman, 1–34. Lanham, MD: Rowman & Littlefield, 1999.

Joachim, H. H. *Aristotle, The Nicomachean Ethics*. Oxford: Clarendon, 1962.

Kenny, Anthony. *The Aristotelian Ethics*. Oxford: Clarendon, 1978.

———. "Happiness." *Proceedings of the Aristotelian Society, New Series* 66 (1965–66) 93–102.

Kraut, Richard. *Aristotle on the Human Good*. Princeton: Princeton University Press, 1989.

———. "Aristotle on the Human Good: An Overview." In *Aristotle's Ethics: Critical Essays*, edited by N. Sherman, 79–104. Lanham, MD: Rowman & Littlefield, 1999.

Liddell, H.G., et al., eds. *A Greek-English Lexicon*. Oxford: Clarendon, 1968.

Long, A. A. "Aristotle on *Eudaimonia*, Nous, and Divinity." In *Aristotle's Nicomachean Ethics: A Critical Guide*, edited by J. Miller, 92–114. Cambridge: Cambridge University Press, 2011.

Majithia, R. "Aristotle on the Good Life." PhD diss., University of Guelph, 1999.

Meyer, S. S. "Living for the Sake of an Ultimate End." In *Aristotle's Nicomachean Ethics: A Critical Guide*, edited by J. Miller, 47–65. Cambridge: Cambridge University Press, 2011.

Nagel, Thomas. "Aristotle on *Eudaimonia*." *Phronesis* 17.3 (1972) 252–59.

Nussbaum, M. C. *The Fragility of Goodness, Luck, and Ethics in Greek Tragedy and Philosophy*. Cambridge: Cambridge University Press, 2001.

Pakaluk, Michael. *Aristotle's Nicomachean Ethics*. Cambridge: Cambridge University Press, 2005.

Paulo, Germaine. "Aristotle's Understanding of the Relation Between Virtue and Friendship." PhD diss., Fordham University, 1996.

Plato. *Republic*. Edited by John M. Cooper. Translated by G. M. A. Grube. Revised by C. D. C. Reeve. Indianapolis: Hackett, 1997.

Price, A. W. *Virtue and Reason in Plato and Aristotle*. Oxford: Oxford University Press, 2011.

Reeve, C. D. C. *Action, Contemplation, and Happiness: An Essay on Aristotle*. Cambridge, MA: Harvard University Press, 2012.

———. "Notes." In *Nicomachean Ethics*, edited by C. D. C. Reeve, 196–354. Indianapolis: Hackett, 2014.

Richardson, Gabriel Ashford. "Happy Lives and the Highest Good, An Essay on Aristotle's Nicomachean Ethics." PhD diss., Princeton University, 2001.

Richardson Lear, Gabriel. "Aristotle on Happiness and Long Life." In *The Quest for the Good Life: Ancient Philosophers on Happiness*, edited by Oyvind Rabbas, et al., 127–45. Oxford: Oxford University Press, 2015.

———. "Happiness and the Structure of Ends." In *A Companion to Aristotle*, edited by Georgios Anagnostopoulos, 387–403. Malden, MA: Blackwell, 2009.

———. *Happy Lives and the Highest Good: An Essay on Aristotle's Nicomachean Ethics*. Princeton: Princeton University Press, 2004.

Roche, T. D. "Happiness and External Goods." In *The Cambridge Companion to Aristotle's Nicomachean Ethics*, edited by R. Polansky, 34–63. Cambridge: Cambridge University Press, 2014.

Roochnik, David. "What is *Theoria*? Nicomachean Ethics Book 10.7-8." *Classical Philology* 104.1 (2009) 69–82.

Ross, David. *Aristotle*. London: Routledge, 1995.

Rowe, Christopher. "Historical Introduction." In *Nicomachean Ethics*, edited by Sarah Broadie and Christopher Rowe, 3–8. Oxford: Oxford University Press, 2002.

Russell, Daniel. *Happiness for Humans*. Oxford: Oxford University Press, 2012.

Sabou, Sorin. *Happiness as Actuality in Nicomachean Ethics: An Overview*. Eugene, OR: Pickwick, 2018.

Scott, Dominic. "Aristotle on the Good Life." In *The Routledge Companion to Ancient Philosophy*, edited by James Warren and Frisbee Sheffield, 347–60. New York: Routledge, 2013.

Shea, J. F. "Happiness and Theorizing in Aristotle's Ethics." PhD diss., University of Pittsburgh, 1986.

Sherman, Nancy. *The Fabric of Character: Aristotle's Theory of Virtue*. Oxford: Clarendon, 1989.

Shields, Christopher. *Aristotle*. London: Routledge, 2014.

———. "Book III." In *De Anima*, edited by Christopher Shields, 255–380. Clarendon Aristotle Series. Oxford: Clarendon, 2016.

Stone, M. A. "An Interpretation of Aristotle's Notion of Happiness in Nicomachean Ethics." PhD diss., Vanderbilt University, 1982.

TLG Workplace 7.0. Silver Mountain Software. CD-ROM.

Urmson, J. O. *Aristotle's Ethics*. Oxford: Blackwell, 1988.

BIBLIOGRAPHY

Van Cleemput, G. "Aristotle on Happiness in the Nicomachean Ethics and the Politics." PhD diss., University of Chicago, 1999.

www.ingramcontent.com/pod-product-compliance
Lightning Source LLC
Chambersburg PA
CBHW070917160426
43193CB00011B/1497